ASIA:
An Expat Adventure

TIMOTHY MARC PELLETIER

AuthorHouse™
1663 Liberty Drive
Bloomington, IN 47403
www.authorhouse.com
Phone: 1-800-839-8640

Published by AuthorHouse 5/7/2013

ISBN: 978-1-4817-4564-2 (sc)
ISBN: 978-1-4817-4617-5 (e)

Library of Congress Control Number: 2013907404

Any people depicted in stock imagery provided by Thinkstock are models,
and such images are being used for illustrative purposes only.
Certain stock imagery © Thinkstock.

This book is printed on acid-free paper.

For my mother, father, and family
Thank you for your unwavering love, guidance, and support.

TABLE OF CONTENTS

ACKNOWLEDGEMENTS

SPECIAL THANKS TO:

Michael Meier, Joshua Davies, Robert Kienzle, and Brendan Alexander

EXTRA SPECIAL THANKS TO:

Czarina, Andy, David, Josh, Bob, Jason, BGA and Terry, Sam Kim, Devon, Vernon, Braham, Jiyeon, Rusty and Lynn, Sook Young Jun, Mi Sun Na, Eunmi Go, Inhee, DK Kenny Lee, Kate, Rose, Alex, Frank, Sam Evans, Jonathan, and Angel for saving my life in China. You all are such wonderful and inspirational people who have changed my life forever.

CREDITS:

Editor: Stephanie Campbell, Massachusetts
Editorial Insight: Michael Meier, MBA, DTM, San Diego, California
Index: Timothy Marc Pelletier
Photos: Timothy Marc Pelletier
Interior Design & Typesetting: AuthorHouse

FOREWORD

By Mike Meier, MBA, DTM
Author of *A FOCUSED PURSUIT in China*

You have made an EXCELLENT decision picking up my friend Tim Pelletier's book *ASIA: An Expat Adventure*. Whether you're planning on teaching in Korea, going on vacation to China, or just reading for your own amusement, this first-person account of living and working abroad I promise will not be like any other!

After working in China in 2009, I met Tim when I started working in South Korea in 2010. Before I had even met him, I saw this Bostonian fiercely compete in a debate sponsored by his local Toastmasters club. After the debate we had dinner with a large group of people, and I got to know this quite interesting individual. His personality THEN was the same as NOW, as you will find in these coming pages: raw and intense, but informative and to the point.

For two years Tim and I had a perpetual dialogue about Asian culture. We both splurged on Korean customs we enjoyed and tried to avoid others we appalled. Our stories always flowed, whether we were discussing harsh and unrealistic business practices (Chapter 3), the unpredictable yet fun dating scene (Chapter 7), and the never-ending saga of learning the Korean language (Chapter 11). At the time of this book's publishing, Tim's in Boston, and I'm in San Diego. But we both still talk regularly, especially about our times overseas.

After successfully publishing my first title, *A FOCUSED PURSUIT in China: 14 Business Tips to Know Before You Go*, Tim came to me about wanting to publish his own book about his experiences in Asia. I told him to go for it, and just to be himself. I loved reading through *ASIA: An Expat Experience* because it feels like Tim is talking to me in some random coffee show, going on in his thick Boston accent! Below is why you are going to read this book in its entirety, and then tell your friends about it.

Can you say "RAW"? Tim's writing style is very in-your-face/no-holds-barred/here's-the-truth-whether-you like-it-or-not. When he's angry, he cusses. When he's frustrated, he specifically writes what is going on in his head. If you greatly appreciate "political correctness," then this book is not for you. But it will keep you entertained and engaged.

No yawning. This is not a textbook to make you fall asleep, but rather a to-the-point lecture. Every chapter, he defines and introduces his theme, throws in some stories and visible examples, and then moves on. It's a simple style, but packs a punch.

The devil is in the details. Some chapters get quite technical, but it is stuff you need to understand. So put on your thinking cap! For instance, I have an MBA, but Tim explains the Korea tax and pension systems like I have never heard before (Chapter 4). I also believe he truly has a photographic memory because the level of detail he can discuss, while not losing me, is quite impressive.

Well, I won't keep you any longer. Get going on Tim's *ASIA: An Expat Adventure.* Maybe soon you will be on a plane to Asia, starting your own "FOCUSED PURSUIT."

Mike Meier, MBA, DTM
San Diego, California
Founder of FOCUSED PURSUIT LLC
www.FOCUSEDPURSUIT.com
www.MikeMeier.us

PRELUDE

In July 2008, I embarked on a journey that would change my life forever. I made the hard choice to leave everything I knew behind and travel into the unknown. A year earlier, I had lost my job as a rental sales manager and, with it, my faith in the United States economy. I had been living way outside my means, had just bought a new car, and found myself unable to pay my bills. My situation seemed rather hopeless, as the only jobs I could find paid only minimum wage or were jobs in struggling restaurants waiting tables or bartending. To try to make things work, I resorted to working two and three jobs, but after six months, my bills were stacked up, and I was absolutely miserable. I needed to do something different, but I didn't know what.

It was my younger brother who gave me the idea to go live abroad and teach English as a second language. I fought the idea for months, hoping things in the U.S. would change, but they didn't. To say it simply, I was afraid to leave my friends, family, and everything I knew behind. With my back against the wall, I decided to take a chance.

I truly think that everything in life happens for a reason and that it was my destiny to go to Asia. This book is a true testament to my adventures over the course of my four years in Asia teaching and traveling through many countries. I learned so many valuable lessons about myself, different cultures, and how beautiful the world really is. I had many mishaps and fumbles along the way, from food poisoning to almost dying. I traveled to several countries in Southeast Asia, living a life most people only dream about. From the United States to South Korea, from the beaches of Thailand to the Great Wall of China, this was my destiny.

It is my hope that through my journey, you'll not only have the desire to travel, but also learn a few things along the way and have a few laughs at my expense.

CHAPTER ONE

The Arrival

To tell you about what it was like arriving in Korea, I have to start at the beginning. I, like many others in the U.S., was laid off humping one crappy job to another just to make ends meet. It, of course, wasn't easy, and I was hitting my head against the wall trying to figure out what I could do. I started substitute teaching and it was pretty good for a while, until thousands of teachers across the state were laid off, and my position became obsolete.

Thanks to my brother and his infinite wisdom, he talked to me about leaving the U.S. and exploring the world. My brother, although younger than me, had traveled a lot of the world through Europe and Africa. He started in college by doing a semester abroad, and then went back to teach and travel. He told me that I could go and live abroad teaching in many foreign countries and how to apply. This had been unbeknownst to me, but I followed his instructions and put my resume on Dave's ESL Café. Dave's ESL Café is a website for teachers who want to teach English as a second language. You can pretty much teach anywhere in the world. Some countries require little to no credentials, and others require a lot. To my surprise, within 24 hours I had about one hundred e-mails from all over the world. With a little bit of research, I found that South Korea was said to have the best pay and living conditions to teach abroad.

I started working with a recruiter and learned that I needed several documents to teach abroad, so I started the process. Two months later, I had all my documents together, including my passport, college diploma, sealed transcripts, criminal record check, and a health statement. Over the course of the next four months, I was offered several jobs that I accepted, but they kept falling through for one reason or another. In retrospect, I think the recruiter was just interested in making as much money as he could by eventually placing me at one of the worst hagwons in Korea. A hagwon is equivalent to an academy in the U.S., but is used for extracurricular education such as learning English or how to play the piano. Recruiters get paid more from hagwons that have a poor reputation, but you can find information about every school on Dave's ESL Cafe.

After five months of waiting, I gave up and actually took a position at a company in the city and forgot about going to Korea. But four weeks later, I got the phone call that would change my life forever. The recruiter called and said, "I've got a job for you."

I said, "Really, like the last twenty offers?"

He said, "I'm serious, and you need to fly out Monday morning at 8:30 a.m."

It was Friday at midnight! Needless to say, I told everyone

I could, packed my bags, had a party, and left everything I knew in the U.S., looking for the next big thing in the land of Kimchi and Samgypsal.

If you don't know how far away Korea is, I'll tell you. It's a twelve to thirteen—hour flight from LA, fifteen hours to NY, and eighteen hours to Boston. That's flying time, never mind the layovers. I can tell you this, the hagwon definitely bought the cheapest ticket it could find to bring me to Korea. It took me two and a half days to get to Korea. I had four layovers, and each was anywhere from six to twelve hours long. I stopped in Pittsburg, Detroit, LA, and Japan and finally landed at Incheon Airport at 10:30 P.M. Wednesday night. I was given the phone number of my new employer to call if I had any problems, but go figure, he didn't speak English and hung up on me when I called. There was also supposed to be someone to pick me up at the airport and take me to my apartment, but I didn't see him. After grabbing my luggage, trying to call my new boss, and having no idea what to do, I started walking around. Eventually I was so stressed out, I walked through the gates and outside to smoke a cigarette. It was the beginning of July, and it had to be 120 degrees with the humidity.

Standing there freaked out, not knowing what to do, I realized that for the first time in my life, I was truly all alone. Halfway around the world, $500 in my pocket, and not a clue what to do, I literally started praying for a miracle. It was at that very moment as I was finishing my cigarette, I looked up and saw that the old adjushi in front of me was holding a shredded piece of cardboard with my last name spelled wrong. Adjushi means old man in Korean, and Adjuma means old woman. I approached him and tried to communicate that the person on the cardboard was me. He proceeded by yelling at me in Korean, and, I think, telling me to go away. I ripped the cardboard from his hands and pointed to both the cardboard and me, showing that we were one and the same. No apologies were given, but he brought me to his van and we made our way to the big city.

Looking out the window, I couldn't help but wonder what was in store for me. Did I make the right choice? Was this going to be a big mistake? I also kept telling myself that this could be the chance of a lifetime. Once we entered the city, I thought I was in Vegas. The bustling city lit up like a Christmas tree. There were neon lights everywhere, tall buildings, and so many people out on the street, I couldn't believe it. I had been to Los Angeles and New York City before, but this was different. It was every street, and everywhere I looked. I was soon to get one of the biggest shocks of my life.

It took quite a long time for the taxi driver to find my apartment. Maybe that is because there is no such thing as a street with a name on it in South Korea. Only streets with numbers, and they all merge together in a mess. After several phone calls, I finally arrived. The funny thing was that it wasn't my boss who greeted me. His 14-year-old daughter came down the hill and walked me up to the apartment. Once I entered, I couldn't believe what I saw. An older Korean man and woman, who I eventually found out were my bosses, were literally using a garden hose to clean the inside of my new apartment. Everything—and I mean everything—was completely soaked. This included every wall, the ceilings and, most importantly, my bed, which I was so desperate to crash on after my long flight.

My new boss handed me my keys, a cell phone that looked like a truck ran it over, and said bye. His daughter translated for him, saying, "He'll be by tomorrow to show you the school."

Off they went, and I immediately picked up the phone and called home. My mother answered and I said, "I'm safe, but you've gotta get me out of here!" She told me to wait it out and give it a few days. And so it started—my Korean experience as an expat. An expat, short for expatriate, is someone who lives outside his or her country, or who has been exiled. This was the beginning of my new existence.

CHAPTER TWO

ESL

My first Korea birthday party held monthly for the students.

Not everyone in the world knows what ESL (English as a Second Language) means, but that's it. There are several different forms of ESL and many different acronyms that are used. I'll do my best to break it down for you and include some stories along the way.

ESL literally means teaching English as a second language to anyone outside an English-speaking country. There are several acronyms that are used and tossed around. ESOL: English for speakers of other languages, EFL: English as a foreign language and EAL: English as an additional language are all widely used terms in regards to learning and teaching English, but are used differently from country to country.

While I was living in Asia, I was teaching English as a second language, commonly known as TESL. English language teaching (ELT) is a widely used term in regards to many different markets and publishing companies around the world. Teaching English as a foreign language (TEFL is probably the most common. Teaching English as a second language (TESL) and teaching English to speakers of other languages (TESOL) and are also used.

What does this all really mean? Well, not too much, really, and in my opinion, I would say that it's all just a bunch of terms. How many different kinds of cereal are there in the supermarkets that are basically the same? If you were to go to college and get a degree to teach English as a second language, it might matter, but in the grand scheme of things when trying to get a job in Asia, experience always counts for more.

If you're thinking of going to live abroad, whether it be to teach or for any reason, it will be the culture difference that affects you more. Teaching English to foreigners might seem a little daunting the first few days, but becomes routine fairly quickly. In most cases, it depends on what level of students you're teaching. Before leaving to go to Korea, I was deathly afraid to teaching kindergarten kids. I didn't want to be changing diapers and wiping noses. To my surprise, it was the younger kids I loved the most. They were all so cute and like little sponges. I won't lie to you and tell you that teaching a class of Korean three-year-olds wasn't hard. Using what little Korean I knew at the time didn't help. However, a year later, when my Korean speaking was better, I found it much easier.

If you're not teaching kindergarten, you'll be surprised how easy it really is. Most of the books I was given to teach from were fairly easy to use, and lesson planning only took a few minutes. Most schools require lesson planning to make sure you're actually teaching in class, although some do not. The schools that I taught at did require lesson planning. It surely is not like lesson planning in the U.S. though, and there is far less paperwork for you to do at the end of the day.

I've been asked several times the difference between teaching in the U.S. and teaching in Korea and China. I always say that it's really difficult to compare because those countries have such a different method of learning than we do. Kids go to school in Asia from 8 a.m. to 10 p.m. Learning is a huge part of their culture, and not just in math and science, but also music and the arts. In Korea, the students I had, with a few exceptions, were very well behaved. In China, I found students to be a little more wise and disrespectful. However, almost all students did well in class in both countries. In the U.S., I always found it difficult to inspire children who had certain behavioral problems. I had worked as a residential counselor and teacher for several years after college and had also been a substitute teacher for several different schools. There always seemed to be one student who would fail everything. I never had this problem in Asia. One main difference would be that children go to school on the weekends in China.

I really did love teaching in Asia. It took me a while to get used to it, but it grew on me. Most days walking into school, I had several kids coming up and hugging me, asking me their latest question in broken English. I was also able to develop relationships with some parents, some of whom I still keep in contact with to this day. I was taken to dinner several times by a couple of different parents, even though it's technically against the rules. It was really nice to actually take the time to get to know them and let them get to know me a little better.

It wasn't only because of the kids, but also because of the natural atmosphere among foreigners, that I loved teaching abroad. Foreigners tended to stick together and help each other out. The several friends I met along the way always made it seem like I was on vacation. In some ways, you really are on vacation, traveling to a new place every weekend. I also took several trips with my school, which helped me learn a lot about Korean culture. It was for all of these reasons that I decided to stay in Asia for a second year.

After my first year, I started working on several different certifications trying to build my resume and get a better job within Seoul. With a little bit of luck, I was able to secure a much better job at a private elementary school. It paid me $2,300 USD a month and it came with five months paid vacation, which wasn't too shabby. It's also the reason I was able to travel so much. I joined Toastmasters International, a club focused on public speaking and leadership skills, and I started taking classes to improve my Korean. On breaks from school, I did my best to travel anywhere I could. I enjoyed my life there so much that I often considered staying forever. That wouldn't be the case, as life has a way of catching up to us, but I'll never forget the times I had.

Timothy Marc Pelletier

Kingdom Of Hyehwa Toastmasters Executive Board

CHAPTER THREE

The First Hagwon
and
All the Bullshit

Coming to Korea to teach English was by far one of the hardest decisions I've ever had to make, but overall both a good and bad decision for many reasons. The first hagwon I worked at was by far one of the worst schools in Korea for several reasons. The following is a true account of what happened to me over the span of a year. It is also in most cases what you can expect to happen to you if you also choose to work at a hagwon in Korea.

Schools in Korea are broken up into many different levels. There are hagwons that are private academies, which generally hold classes for kindergarten in the morning and grade school through high school in the afternoon and evening. Hagwons in general are open from 8 a.m. to 10 p.m. Monday to Saturday. There are also private schools, language schools, elementary, middle, and high schools, music schools, and sports schools. Pretty much anything you can think of will have some sort of school or hagwon that you can go to. In my opinion, there are more hagwons than regular schools, and in general, most foreigners end up working at one of these schools their first year.

At first, like anything new, there was a learning curve I needed to get over. I had never taught English as a second language before, but I did, however, have years of experience working with children in the U.S. I graduated with a degree in psychology and worked in one of the top psychiatric centers for children for six and a half years. I also substitute taught off and on through college and after for extra money. It always came natural to me. Maybe because my mother was a teacher, and she always said I was meant to be a teacher. In my interview with this hagwon before coming, the manager only asked if I loved children. My answer, of course was yes, and I was hired.

My first day on the job was extremely weird, and I was introduced to so many people that I had no idea what was going on. All the introductions were also done in Korean, and I therefore understood nothing. There was absolutely no training involved other than "these are your books and this is your schedule." The kids overall were not bad and generally just laughed every time I talked. The level of English among Korean students is generally higher than one would expect, but what we might call broken English like, "I go bathroom." Some older students had a high English proficiency. Eventually, the students actually started listening to me, and I began teaching. I asked several questions, some of which were answered, and I was on my way. It got much worse from here on out, but this is the nature of hagwons in Korea.

Teaching at a good hagwon means there actually is an

established curriculum that you teach from, and you will be trained for a few days. You can also tell by how much you see the owner in the school. A lot of hagwons are only run as moneymaker businesses. The parents have to pay a great deal of money to send their children there. Usually it's the equivalent of a couple thousand dollars a month per student. The problem with teaching at a bad hagwon is that most are glorified babysitting institutions where, although you are expected to teach, it's only half at best of what you do. A lot of these hagwons are places where parents send their kids because they are either working or don't want to take care of them. Also, the parents only care if their children are doing poorly, and if they are, it is completely your fault. It's a total oxymoron, but the more you care about how well a child is doing, the more wrong you are. I can't tell you how many times I reported that a child never did his homework or that she failed a test, and every time it was dismissed. But, when report cards come out, that child better have the best grade in the class. It is also a normal occurrence for the manager of the school to change the grades of a student to stop the parents from getting upset.

One time, a student of mine went home and complained to his mother that I gave him a timeout for not doing his homework. In fact, he was given a timeout for not following simple directions in class. His mother actually spoke decent English and came to the school to talk to me about her son. The basics were this: Her son was the worst behaved kid in the class. He never did his homework or class work, and was always distracting the other students. I had reported all of this to the manager and assumed the mother knew all of these issues. I was so wrong! I talked to her about her son, and she was completely shocked. She then went and tore my manager a new ass, who then tore me a new ass for being honest with the mother. You see, it's all about money, and if that mother pulls her son from the school, it becomes my fault as the teacher for the school losing money. As for the money paid to the teachers, that's a totally different story.

I know in the U.S. we are accustomed to working a normal schedule of eight hours a day and everything else is overtime. In Korea, it is expected of you to work for a salary because your boss truly makes you work extra hours and will never pay you overtime. My contract stated that I was required to teach twenty-five hours a week. My actual schedule was from 10 a.m. to 7:30 p.m. I was there those hours Monday through Friday. If you add it up, that's forty-seven and a half hours a week. I questioned this after my first week and was told. "That's why you have breaks." The problem with breaks is that you can't leave the school. I said, "Well, I have to be here, so how is it a break?" There was no answer given.

Eventually, things continued to get harder and harder. My classes began to change weekly, and I was required to write a lesson plan for each class that I taught. I was writing lesson plans for classes, and then using lesson plans that other teachers had written when the classes changed. The whole point of writing a lesson plan is so that you have a plan and are familiar with the material. I was always confused and always in the wrong classroom with the wrong books. It was mass confusion almost all of the time.

I also slowly began to be given more classes during the times that I was supposed to have breaks. I asked, "Why am I teaching more hours than what my contract stated?" and I was yelled at for asking so many questions. Teaching at a hagwon, in my opinion, is really just a trap. The school owns your visa, pays you 15 days after the month finishes, never tells you very much at all, and everything is done at the last minute. Looking back on it now, I wonder why I put up with so much, but I honestly didn't know any better. I thought all schools were like the one I was at. Eventually, I found out that working at a hagwon was the worst job you could have and that hagwons were known for treating people horribly. This kind of knowledge came from experience and by talking with other expats that had been there longer and knew the truth of it all.

In Korean contracts, you are given a monthly salary, and upon completion of a year contract, you are supposed to get a month's salary bonus and a plane ticket home paid for. For me, I couldn't have been happier that my time with this school had come to an end. Unfortunately, I had to refuse to teach the last couple of days just so that I could get most of the money that was owed to me. In the end, I still lost out, because although I got my plane ticket and the majority of my money, the owner still to this day owes me about $2,000 USD. Included in that is eight days of vacation pay, part of my last month's salary, and reimbursement from money he kept to pay my bills.

There were several other problems I had at this hagwon over the course of the year, but most were non-teaching related. You can read about them in the next couple of chapters.

Hagwon Scams

When choosing to live and work in a foreign country, it is very important that you understand your rights and the laws that protect you. The information is out there if you want it, but in a lot of cases, it takes time to find. Websites like Dave's ESL are great for helping you if you're teaching. You can also use Google, which has been a lifesaver for me in many ways. Hagwons in Korea try to pull many scams against foreigners. Over the last three years of teaching in Korea, I've learned most of them, but I'm never surprised when I hear a new one.

Hagwons, or any school, for that matter, in Korea, are required by law to pay you directly in full to your bank account minus taxes, pension, and insurance. This is important to know because a lot of school owners will try to pay you in cash to create inaccuracies. Owners are not allowed to take money out for your bills and are not allowed to hold your money if they feel you owe money for certain bills or anything. Your salary is to be deposited in your account on the day stated in your contract without question. If you are told differently, you are being lied to, and they are breaking the Korean law. A lot of hagwons get away with these scams because it's very difficult to report and fight them to get your money. There is a court process that can take place, but in most cases it takes months before any due process is given. Therefore, most teachers just leave or start a new job.

Here is a description of some of the scams you will hear. There are many variations, and if it sounds weird, it probably is a scam of sorts.

By Korean law, the owner of any school is required to take a portion of your pay for taxes. In most cases it is 3.3 percent. It's not much, and you can file a tax return in Korea and get most of it back. The hagwon owners will take this money out of your pay, but never send that money to the tax office. Then, when you go to file your taxes, you are told that you have no account and that you owe the tax office. This happened to me, and in fact, I didn't learn about filing taxes until my second year in Korea. The second school I worked at was actually a really great private school that was awesome when it came to paperwork and doing things by the book. That school filed my taxes for me, and instead of getting what I thought would be a decent amount of money back, I ended up receiving 74,000 KRW (Korean Won) or $70 USD for two years' worth of taxes. I was pissed, to say the least! The tax office said that I owed an entire year worth of taxes and kept 85 percent of my tax return.

When it comes to pension, the scam is roughly the same but with a bit of a twist. Pension is 4.5 percent of your pay taken out monthly. The owner of the school is supposed to match this amount equally, making the total paid 9 percent. If you are getting paid the average 2.2 million KRW a month, that equals to 198,000 KRW a month. Times that by twelve months, and you get 2,376,000 KRW. That's roughly $2,100 USD. That's a lot of money for someone to take from you. You can check to see if your school is paying your pension easily by using Google and looking up what pension office is closest to you and calling. You'll need your alien ID card number and that's it. If your school isn't paying, you can tell the pension office to contact your school to set up your account and pay the money owed to you.

Another variation of this is the owner telling the pension office that you are making half of what you actually are. This allows the school to pay less money or nothing at all by literally just taking your money and paying the office. The only way you can find out is by calling the pension office. In this case, you should always have a copy of your contract that states your salary right on it.

When it comes to health insurance in Korea, you have to have it. You may be the lucky one that never gets sick, but if you do, you had better have insurance. Hagwon owners will not talk to you about your insurance unless you ask for it. They will, however, deduct it from your paycheck. It's not hard to set up your insurance, and it will be retroactive to your start date. Once you get your alien ID card, you can get insurance and the school owner has to set it up for you. If you've been to the doctor before you get your insurance card, you can just go back and get a refund.

Paying your bills in Korea can be an absolute nightmare. It all seems really easy when talk to you about it over the phone or by e-mail. A lot of schools will advertise that they pay for everything, but don't. At my first hagwon, I had to pay for my gas heat, hot water, electrical, and my cell phone. The first problem is that the bills are all in Korean, of course, so understanding what they say is impossible. I want to give you the basic strategies of what to do so you don't get screwed like I did. Do not make the mistake of asking your owner what it says. He won't give you a straight answer in most cases. Instead, the first thing to do is copy every single bill, letter, and notice that you get in the mail. Do this regardless of whether you know what it says. Anybody can look at the bill and figure out that it says a numbered amount at the top. The next thing is to have someone show you where and how to pay all of your bills directly. Do not pay your school to pay the bills for you. Your bills in Korea for the most part should never exceed 300,000 KRW ($250 USD) a month, and that's in the winter when it's cold. It your bills seem really high, something is wrong and you're either paying for someone else or you gave your boss the money and he didn't pay your bill. Another problem is that a lot of bills take more than month to come in. You might get your first bills two months after you start working.

Another scam I learned at my first hagwon was that the school owner gave me a cell phone that was on a joint account with his entire family. There were five phones being used on the account. I was paying for all five, and I was paying for all of them for five months. I found this out by mistake because I was out one night and lost my phone. To get it replaced, I needed the school owner to come to the phone shop with me. The clerk, who happened to speak a little English, asked me which phone number it was. I said, "There's only one number," and he told me that there were five phone numbers on the account. I first got a new phone and then went back to the store without the school owner after completely figuring it out, and asked what portion of the bills were mine. I, in fact, was paying more than 100,000 KRW instead of 30,000 KRW like I should have been. When I confronted the owner and school manager, they lied to me and said my bills were from calling home so much. This was impossible because I used Skype to call home. Even though I stood my ground, I was never refunded that money. I demanded, however, that the phone be put in my name only on a completely separate account. It was done, and by miraculous surprise, my next month's bill was 27,000 KRW. In simple math, 100,000 KRW is about $90 USD. I lost about $250 USD due to this scam.

Another scam that my school had going was that the electric bill for my apartment, which was owned by my hagwon owner. There were three apartments, and I was on the third floor. I liked my apartment because, although small, it was bigger than most one-room apartments. I had two rooms plus a bathroom. I was also lucky enough to have a wrap-around balcony that overlooked the city where I worked. The problem was that both the second and third floors shared an electric meter. He worked it out with the second floor that their electric bill was included in their rent, but what did he care? I was actually paying the bill for both floors for about seven months.

You see, once you live in another country for a while, you begin to get wise of your surroundings and what's normal. When you tell someone your cell phone bill is 150,000 KRW a month and that person looks at you like you have ten heads, you know something is wrong. I started asking lots of questions, and before I knew it, I actually had a decent understanding of what was going on right in front of me and how naive I actually was. Some of the best advice I can give you is to trust no one. Not even a foreigner at first. Eventually you figure it out and know who you can trust. As for trusting Korean hagwon owners, just don't do it. You'll always be a foreigner in their eyes, and from books that I've read about Korean culture and business, the rule of thumb is that you will get your head chopped off if you leave it out there.

The Pipes Bursting

When living in a foreign country, your home becomes your sanctuary. It's the place you go not only to rest but also to forget that you're not in Kansas anymore. Living abroad can be tough because you have to deal with everything differently, and there is a lot of extra pressure on you all the time due to cultural problems and occurrences. Nothing is ever as it seems, and trying to solve what to you is easy becomes extremely difficult when living abroad. For instance, when I realized that there were some problems with the plumbing in my apartment, I told my school. The school owner felt that ignoring the problem would make it go away, and he was wrong.

I had been living in Korea for approximately three months or so when the plumbing in my bathroom started to get really bad. I continued to complain, and my school owner kept saying, "Don't worry about it." The problem was that the apartment was owned by the school. It was old, and the owner of my hagwon was a cheap degenerate prick who didn't want to spend the money to fix the problems in the apartment. It was only the plumbing! Half the electrical sockets didn't work. There was exposed wiring, and the wallpaper was tearing off the concrete walls. The locks on all the windows were broken, and there was that shared electricity problem. I tried not complaining about the little things, but when every day you go home to see water all over the floor in the bathroom, which eventually after time began leaking into the kitchen as well, I knew this was something that had to be fixed. My dad is a general contractor, so I know a thing or two when it comes to plumbing and electrical.

As I'm sure you can guess, eventually all hell broke loose and the pipes finally burst. I was out late one night on a Friday with some friends and having a good time in Itaewan. As always, we were drinking quite heavily and I eventually needed to go home. It was around 3 a.m. Upon entering my apartment, I was mortified by what I saw. First, when I opened my door, water came pouring out of the apartment, soaking my shoes. At some point in the night, the pipes had burst and continued pouring water into the apartment. Apartments in Korea are made of concrete, so there was no place for the water to go. Not even the small drain in the bathroom could keep up with the flow of water. Like any smart person, I turned off the water and began trying to mop as much water up as I could. In my estimate, I think there was about three inches of water in the three separate rooms of my apartment—luckily not enough to reach the electrical sockets. It took me all night to clean up the water, and around 8 a.m., I was exhausted and so pissed off I could have killed someone that looked at me the wrong way. I called my supervisor and explained what had transpired. She then called the hagwon owner and told him what happened. The cheap prick bastard actually had the nerve to tell me that it was my fault and that I had to fix it, call a plumber, and pay for it myself.

"It's not my fucking fault!" I told my manager.

She said she didn't know what to do. I, of course, mentioned that I had been complaining about this for months to be fixed and that now the pipes finally broke. She admitted that I was right, but still said that I had to fix it. You can imagine how pissed off I was. How can you tell the building owner for months to fix something and then have him tell you it's your fault when something seriously goes wrong?

I at this point called one of my friends that was Korean, but had lived in the U.S. for six years as an exchange student. I had him take me to a plumbing supply store and bought all the parts to repair the pipes in the bathroom. I was actually surprised at how cheap the parts were, and the store owner actually gave me a pipe wrench to borrow. Looking back on the incident, I realized that not everything in a foreign country is bad; there are always good people willing to help you, too.

It took me all day to go get the parts, replace all the piping for the sink in the bathroom and return the wrench to the plumbing store. The parts cost about 50,000 KRW or $45 USD, and it took about six hours to take everything apart and put it all back together.

Monday when I returned to school, I demanded to be reimbursed for not only the plumbing parts, but also for the labor I had to put in to fix the pipes. I was basically laughed out of his office, and I told him I was quitting unless he paid me. I ending up getting paid for the parts, but not all the time and suffering I had to go through over the weekend. I also had to deal with the hagwon owner being a total asshole for the next three weeks because he had to pay me for the parts.

I was not happy with him, my school manager, or anything that had to do with Korea. Unfortunately, this is one of those circumstances that anyone could go through in life, but living abroad and having it happen makes it all the more difficult due to the language barrier and frustration. I'm not sure that there wasn't any way I could have avoided this from happening, but I learned that some things are just out of your control.

CHAPTER SIX

The Dentist

Before coming to Korea, like most people I had some dental work done in the previous years—a few cavities filled and two molars pulled rather than getting a root canal. Dental work in the U.S. to me is just a routine thing that most people dread because it costs a lot, and it's usually accompanied by pain before, during, after, or all three combined. This is a true account of my experience in Korea and the turmoil I had to go through to get one tooth repaired.

One day while on a lunch break from school, I went to the corner bakery to get a coffee and a bagel. This was a normal thing for me due to not liking a majority of the food that was served at the school. After getting my coffee and bagel, I sat down at a table and began to chomp away. On the third bite, I felt a pop in my mouth. Lo and behold, it was followed by pain. One of the molars in my mouth had broken in half. The truth of it all was that the filling in my tooth had come out a long time prior to this, and I didn't know it. It was only a matter of time until something happened. Of course, something finally did—and of course, that something happened in Korea.

Dentists in Korea are actually rather cheap, or maybe it is best to just say that they are cheaper than in the U.S. A standard root canal and crown in the U.S. can cost anywhere from $1,000 to $3,000. In Korea it typically costs around $500,000 KRW. That's roughly $450 USD as you know it. I knew this after talking with a few people and trusted the advice of my school to go to a dentist that was close by. This was my first mistake. Never trust your school when they advise you to go someplace close. The whole motive is for you to be away from school for less time, rather than get the best care. Either way, I went to see the dentist, and I was lucky enough that he spoke some English. He gave me a normal check up, X-rayed the tooth, and told me I needed a root canal, post, and a crown to repair the tooth. I asked him how much that would cost, and he said about 500,000 KRW. Lucky me, right? Wrong I was.

The next day I went in for my first appointment. It started with him cleaning up the tooth, and then the root canal. He said it would take three visits to finish, and then he could do the post and the crown. It didn't really work out that way. After three visits, I was still in agony and pain. Each visit he seemed to clean and repack the root canal with resin gauze. I couldn't eat anything and my mouth was throbbing constantly. It affected everything I did, from sleeping, to working, to talking—everything, really. I continued to go back to this dentist for treatment for three weeks. The pain continued to the point that I couldn't take it anymore. My friend Dave, with whom I had worked the previous year, also needed a root canal and went to a different dentist. It took only three days and he was never in pain. I decided that something was definitely wrong and, upon returning to the dentist, demanded my money back. It, of course, was a yelling and screaming match, which ended in me getting my money refunded after I said I would sue him.

That same day I went to a different dentist who studied in New York, and I was in for a massive shock. He was recommended by my friend Josh, who I should have asked for advice in the first place. Josh and I met through my friend Andy, who owned and operated a restaurant in Hyewha called the Comfort Zone. We over time became good friends, as we were both in Korea as ESL teachers.

The first dentist I went to fucked up my mouth, to say the very least. First, he drilled through the bottom of the root of my tooth, leaving a hole in my jaw. This caused a major abscess. No wonder I was in so much pain. "What a fucking idiot," I thought to myself. The new dentist, after showing me this through the X-ray he took, said that I needed immediate oral surgery. The dollar signs immediately started flashing before me. It cost a little over 1,000,000 KRW to fix the abscess in my jaw. I then had to wait three weeks for it to heal, while taking painkillers and antibiotics to stop any infection. The good news was I was no longer in any pain. Three weeks later I went for two more visits and I finally had my tooth fully repaired. I ended up with a post and a gold crown. All in all, it cost me about 2,000,000 KRW or $2,000 USD to get a root canal, post, and crown.

The moral of the story is this: Never trust anyone while living in a foreign country, especially someone from your school who is not a foreigner. My best advice would be to ask a foreigner who is your friend, who has lived in the country a long time. A foreigner will almost certainly tell you how it is in a language you can understand. Your health and well-being is always of the utmost importance. Don't let someone else's agenda ever get in the way of that. You'll also probably save yourself a great deal of money.

CHAPTER SEVEN

Dating

I can't lie to you and tell you that one reason I went to Korea wasn't because of the women. I, in fact, as my mother would tell you, have had Asian fever, yellow fever, or whatever you want to call it, since I was ten. It all started due to going to a hair salon where I saw a beautiful Asian model on a poster and told my mom, "I want to marry a girl like that." I guess I was destined since that point on.

I never got the chance to date an Asian girl until after I graduated college. Her name was Malinda, and she was absolutely the most beautiful girl I had ever seen. I did everything in my power to start dating her, and we were together for three years before I eventually screwed it up due to extenuating circumstances and me just being an absolute idiot. She married someone else, and well, I eventually moved on. That was 2003, and it was five years later in July of 2008 that I moved to Korea.

If you think the rumors are true that all Asian girls love Americans or white foreigners, you're wrong, and stay home if that's your reason for going to another country. I've been to several countries through Southeast Asia, and everyone I've talked to has said that most Asians consider foreigners to be arrogant, egotistical, and demanding. They love our money, though, so they'll be nice to you—most of the time.

It wasn't long before I first starting dating in Korea. Or maybe I should say: going out and trying to pick up a beautiful Korean girl. I'm not going to say I'm the most attractive guy out there, and I'm definitely not the ugliest. Generally speaking, I'm just your average Joe, and I was living in Korea. I tried talking to several Korean girls and most of the time was shot down. You see, Korean girls know that foreigners like them, but they're not going to necessarily make it easy for you. Also, it all depends on what you're looking for. There are whole bunch of factors that play in here. I'll start by telling you the basics.

If you want to meet a girl, the bar is definitely not the right place in Korea, unless all you're looking for is a cheap meaningless relationship. You're better off to meet a Korean girl through friends or various clubs and organizations. Sitting in a coffee shop studying Korean and asking a pretty lady for help also works, too. The bar scene in Korea is crazy, and every Korean girl—or most of them anyway—has been hit on a million times. Every bar is like something out of a Project X movie. It really is a numbers game, but anyone can tell you that. If you ask 100 girls if you could buy them a drink, one is bound to say yes! If your priority is to go to Korea and be the bastard foreigner they think you are, all the power to you, but the repercussions will most likely be that at some point, it will come back to you.

The main thing I found in dating in Korea was that it wasn't until I truly tried to understand the culture that things started to make sense, at least a little anyway. I read a book or two and started studying the language. It means a lot when you can say "hello" and "how are you?" in the native tongue. At least you try, and it goes a long way, believe me.

I met the first girl I dated in Korea while out with a buddy, Andy, who will forever be a close friend. We were at JJ's Sports Bar, and these two cute girls were talking to this rich guy that we were with. He got up, leaving his wallet on the bar, and said, "Have whatever you want." Andy and I approached from behind and were talking to the two girls. They bought us a drink—with our friend's money, mind you—and the night progressed with laughs and jokes, as both of them spoke moderate English. We left with them and went back to my buddy Andy's bar/restaurant for a few more drinks, and the girls eventually went home, but not before handing over their numbers. This was great for me as I finally was going to get the chance to date a Korean girl.

It didn't last long, a couple of months, really. We went on dates, and most of the time it was a major struggle to communicate. I'm a strong believer that the most important part of any relationship is communication. I eventually realized that not only did I not understand this girl at all, but she also didn't understand me, either. Culturally we were very different, and where I was very open-minded as an American, so I thought, she was a very conservative Korean. The truth of the matter is this: Cultural differences are extremely hard to overcome. Just having a meaningful conversation can be difficult. To truly date a person from another culture, I think that both people have to have lived abroad in some way, shape or form. It's just easier to communicate and understand each other. This is why from that point forward, one of my first questions to a girl I met was, "Have you ever lived abroad?"

I was single for a while after that. That's not to say that there weren't a few occurrences here and there over the next couple of months. In the spring of 2009, I met who I thought was going to be the girl of my dreams. I was out drinking with some friends of mine in my favorite place, The Comfort Zone in Hyewha, and they decided to go home early. I was drunk and wanted to stay out, so I decided to walk around. I went to this nice little dive called The Flair Bar and decided to go in. I had been there once before, and I remembered that it had this flaming fire show. I sat at the bar, ordered my Jack and Coke, and carried on a conversation with the bartender, whose English was excellent. It just so happened that the girl next to me turned around and engaged in the conversation. Before long it was just us talking. She happened to be with a Japanese friend who I thought was her boyfriend. So I asked, "Is that your boyfriend?" She said, "No, no, just a friend."

We continued to talk over drinks for about two more hours until about 4 am. She handed me her business card and said to give her a call. I waited a few days and then took her out to dinner. From that point forward, our relationship grew.

There's a saying in Korea that every Korean girl who dates a foreigner also has a Korean boyfriend. I'm not sure how true this really is, but what I can tell you is that after a while, I did get an uneasy feeling. Some things just never added up, I guess. We dated for about nine months. For the most part it was OK, but there were also some serious problems. The first was she was deathly afraid of meeting my friends, thinking her English wasn't good enough. The second was that she was so busy with work, we sometimes went weeks without seeing each other. Third, the intimacy part of the relationship completely disappeared. I also began to not trust her for various reasons. She was always late and never said where she was going to be. All in all we broke up, and I used a trip to Thailand to get over the whole situation. We, however, still have an ongoing friendship to this day, and keep in contact through Facebook and e-mail.

The next girl I dated truly pulled the wool right over my eyes. I was basically what you called a trophy boyfriend to her, and she knew how to play the game quite well. There are a lot of girls in Korea who will just date a foreigner to practice their English or because people will look at them when they walk down the street. And that is exactly what this girl wanted from me. It was all great for about two months. Nothing was wrong at all. To me, I thought it was a great relationship. Her English was great, and we had a lot of the same interests and even a few mutual acquaintances. It was at this two-month point where she absolutely fell off the face of the Earth. There was no "fuck you" or "you're an asshole." I tried to contact her for weeks until I finally gave up. In fact, I still to this day have never been given a clear explanation. But, I was told from a friend after that she started dating, or allegedly started dating, a Korean guy immediately after me. I also found out that she was studying for a conversation test in English. This was also the same girl that told me on several occasions she thought we were perfect together and she had never met anyone that treated her as well as I did. The point is that I was just a trophy boyfriend and someone she could use. This was a hard lesson to learn, but it made me wiser, and that was the last time I fell for that trap.

I waited a long time to get involved again. I stayed focused with other things and didn't want to date a Korean girl. Unfortunately, though, even though there are some hot, great, down-to-earth white girls in Korea, I never could find where they hung out. The last Korean girl I met and dated turned out to be a great friend and someone I thought I would always be able to look to for truth and guidance. It didn't end up that way, but maybe that's just the nature of life. To this day, I still live by certain principals she taught me to live by.

CHAPTER EIGHT

Traveling

The Cove on Koh Pi Pi, Thailand

The best part about living in Korea by far had to be the central location and being able to travel. You could say that there are better locations to live in that allow you to travel throughout Asia, but Korea was great for me—not only for me, but also for every other person I knew in Korea. You can go just about anywhere in Asia you want with very few hassles. It also helps to have a great travel agent. I used Zenith Travel. My travel agent, Wystan, was by far the best travel agent ever. He always got me the cheapest and fastest tickets possible. He also was right there waiting when I called him at 8 a.m. needing to change my flight because I woke up too late from having a night of drinking with my friends.

I don't know what you were told growing up, but if you're like me and how I was, you were told that your country was the best, and nothing is better. I'm here to tell you, "Fuck all that shit!" Get out into the world and make up your own mind. Traveling is the best way to do this, but I didn't have to leave Korea to travel—Korea has many wonderful places to visit as well. Just to visit Korea in itself would be a trip. It has beautiful architecture, a killer nightlife, palaces, temples, and lots of history. I learned more, though, once I traveled to Thailand, Japan, Hong Kong, Macau, and the Philippines.

The first trip I made, other than going home to visit my family, was to Thailand for five weeks. I went all by myself, and I honestly think there is no better way to travel. I say this because when you're on your own, you have nothing but time to meet people, experience the culture, and think about it. The world in which you live is a bubble, and until you step outside of that bubble and experience the world for what it truly is, you'll always be naive. When you walk the streets of Bangkok and see the poor everywhere, it will humble you. When you see how beautiful a country can be, but where prostitution is everywhere because that's the only way people know how to feed their families, you might begin to understand what I'm talking about. Thailand is an amazing country. It also is as cheap as cheap can be. Where else can you get a two-hour massage with a happy ending for $12 USD? I went scuba diving on Koh Tao Island for two weeks, made 15 dives, got certified as an advanced diver, and had a bungalow on the beach included for under $400 USD. The diving itself was amazing. Beautiful, crystal—clear visibility, and tons of fish and sea creatures everywhere. You can even go diving with sharks on Shark Island, but you better have your balls screwed on tight for that dive. Are you serious? You can't beat that anywhere as far as I know, but maybe there is a place I haven't been to that offers something similar. There are full moon parties with every drug you can think of to celebrate whatever it is you want to celebrate. May it be some killer bud, or a mushroom shake, if you want it they have it. I didn't do it all, but many people I was with did. And, it was an awesome time, to say the least.

There is something else to be said about Thailand, and that is its natural beauty. It has cascading cliffs and beautiful beaches everywhere. There are ancient temples and ruins thousands of years old. Not to mention the crazy monkeys that will steal your water bottles as you trek through the jungle. You can ride elephants, and you can play with tigers. It was by far my favorite country to visit. The people in Thailand are also the friendliest out of any country I visited. They were always accommodating and willing to help in any way possible to make me happy.

I traveled to Hong Kong and Macau with a great friend of mine, CZ. She's a great companion, and we had a great trip. Hong Kong and Macau are nothing like Thailand. They are warm, sunny and beautiful, but they don't have the natural beauty that Thailand has, in my opinion. Hong Kong and Macau are beautiful, but in other ways. Hong Kong has amazing buildings and architecture. It also has a great nightlife with places to go and party it up in the city like Lang Kwai Funhg and Soho, and there are many others. There are great shopping centers, and everything is cheaper in Hong Kong in regards to clothing. Some things are expensive, though, like transportation and food. Hong Kong is a big metropolitan city, so in some ways it very similar to places like NYC or LA. I recommend seeing the Harbor Lights and the Boulevard of Stars. Go to Victoria Peak and eat at Bubba Gump's. Also see the Big Buddha. Those were my three favorites.

Macau was great, but I didn't get to see as much as I wanted to due to time. It looks much like a mini Las Vegas. There are some old historical sites and really cheap beef jerky that is absolutely delicious. You can also get a tour guide to show you around all day for like ten bucks. It's a good way to save time and get some free samples of things along the way.

The Philippines was my second favorite place to go. I didn't go to Cebu or Borracai, even though they're the most popular tourist places to visit. I went to Coron Town, which is in the southern part near the Palawan Islands. I went there because it is secluded and peaceful, with not a lot of tourists, and has some of the best places to go wreck diving. I became a scuba enthusiast in my travels, and Coron has some amazing diving. If you like scuba diving, I totally recommend it. It was also very cheap. I made 15 dives here over five days, and I had a great instructor named Mike who pushed it to the limits with me, teaching me as much as he could with the time allowed. There's nothing like diving 43 meters deep, swimming through bulkheads, and seeing tank and bulldozers that have been underwater for 60 years. All the while, you can dive through shallow waters and see other shipwrecks at 15 meters with amazing coral and fish everywhere. The visibility was incredible. I also got to swim for a good five minutes with a rather large sea turtle that was just as curious about me as I was of him. To top it off, we dived a volcanic pool that was amazing. It's really indescribable, but the colors and transference between the temperatures was something out of an acid trip.

Coron Town is a peaceful place that gets most of it money from tourism, I would gather. It has a decent nightlife on the low-key side, but great restaurants and places to hang out and watch the sun set across the water. On the down side, there are a lot of very poor people that live in this area. It will definitely make you feel strange in some ways, but humble, and wishing you could do something to help. I definitely would like to go back there again someday and do it all again.

As I stated before, traveling is the best part of living abroad. It allows you to put life into perspective and to be thankful for everything you have in life. It will make you a better person and change you without you even realizing it.

Hong Kong Skyline from Victoria Peek

CHAPTER NINE

Hospitals

One major thing that comes into play when living abroad is health care. Before leaving to go to Korea, I didn't even think that it was a big deal. I usually didn't get sick and hardly ever needed to go to the hospital for anything. Each school I worked for offered insurance, as it was required in each country I lived in. Unfortunately, although much cheaper, the hospitals in Asia for the most part are a pale comparison to those in the U.S. There are also several cheap clinics that people go to first.

After a couple of weeks living in Korea, I got my first experience being sick abroad. If you ever have traveled, you might know that in certain countries just drinking the water can get you sick. The problem with this is that if you live in that country, just things like getting a soda with ice in it can make you sick. One night I just didn't feel well, and the next day I couldn't even leave my bathroom floor. I had dysentery! Dysentery is an inflammatory disorder of the intestine. Caused by any kind of infection, it results in severe diarrhea, fever, and abdominal pain. It's easy to get, and most people who move to another country get this within the first month. I was home sick for two days, and my manager told me to come to the school so the owner could take me to the hospital.

I must have looked like hell when I got there, but my boss took me to the clinic in the building next door to my school. The doctor spoke a little English, and after I explained what my symptoms were, he simply said, "No problem." I was a little confused, but a couple minutes later, a nurse came in and gave me a shot in the ass. It hurt like hell, and the doctor told me I'd have trouble walking for a few hours, but to go home and rest and I'd feel better tomorrow. I'm not sure what he gave me, but I felt like a million dollars the next day.

The second time I got sick was when I was traveling in Thailand. Thailand was awesome, and everything was so cheap and delicious—especially the street food. This was my first mistake. It's very easy to get food poisoning from eating street food, mainly because the vendors don't always cook it properly, or it's been out in the sun too long. Street food is not properly regulated in Thailand. It was a couple of weeks into my trip in Thailand that I started to feel a little funny. A couple of hours later, I was once again hugging a toilet bowl. In Thailand there are very few hospitals outside the major cities. The villages have very small clinics with a cross outside and really aren't prepared to help anyone with a serious problem. I had food poisoning, and that was the first problem. The second problem was that the food poisoning turned into a gastric infection. The third problem was the gastric infection irritated the dormant kidney stones I had at the time, and I was one hurting unit.

I went to the clinic, but there really wasn't much the doctor could do. He prescribed me some painkillers and sent me on my way, recommending that I wait two weeks and then go to

41

the hospital in Korea. I followed his advice, and the painkillers took care of most of my symptoms. When I returned to Korea, the first thing I did was go to the hospital.

Once I arrived at the hospital, I went to the emergency room and stated my symptoms. I guess this is where it gets interesting, but imagine trying to tell some lady in broken English and Korean that you got food poisoning and a gastric infection in Thailand and that you also had kidney stones. The nurse asked me what my symptoms were, and I told her extreme abdominal pain radiating through to the groin area. Not pleasant—and she probably thought I had an STD to go along with it.

Once in the emergency room, it only got worse. The doctors knew I had a serious infection after taking blood samples and asked me if I was allergic to any medicine. I told them no, and they proceeded to do a prick test to check if I was allergic to the medicine they wanted to give me. "If a little red bubble appears, you're allergic," the nurse told me. Well, there really wasn't a bubble, but there was a decent red spot. I didn't even have a chance to object before the nurse gave me this huge injection into my IV anyway, and about 20 seconds later I went into severe anaphylactic shock. It was so bad my heart stopped, and they had to do CPR to revive me. Ceftriaxone, an antibiotic heavily used in Korea was what they had given me. I had never had it before and had no idea I was allergic. I ended up spending the night, thanks to that fiasco, and the next day I had several appointments at the hospital with different specialists.

I first had several X-rays done. Then, I had to see an urologist, who told me that he needed further test results to see how far the infection had spread. He sent me for an ultrasound of my entire abdomen and groin area. As they wheeled me into to this room, there were three nurses in front of me. Two were male and one female, all around 23 to 25 years old. The two males read the chart, handed it to the girl and left the room. How humiliating for me as she covered me in lubricant and moved the machine around. I might have quite enjoyed it, had it been under different circumstances.

After going back to the urologist, he explained that the medicine I got in Thailand was not good enough and that it only held the infection from getting worse. He then checked my prostate gland, which, of course wasn't pleasant, and said he would prescribe me some medicine to take care of the problem. Thankfully, about a week later, I was back to normal, but it was one hell of an ordeal—all over eating some bad street food. My advice, be careful what you eat!

When it comes to hospitals in Asia, an international hospital will always take better care of you, but will cost you more money. I would recommend it, though. After my ordeal at the hospital, I never went back to that one. The next time I was sick, I instead went to Yonsei University Hospital, and the staff took much better care of me. It was an international hospital that would later save my life in China.

CHAPTER TEN

Adjumas and Adjushis

If you've never been to Korea, then you probably have no idea what adjumas (old or married woman) or adjushis (old or married man) means, but now you do. I'm going to tell you all about this because I've probably complained and heard more complaints about this than any other thing in Korea. I'm not really sure why it is this way, but it just is what it is for various reasons and cultural norms in Korea. I'll start by telling you about the adjumas.

Adjumas in Korea can be the sweetest or the meanest old women on the planet. I've had old women smile at me or curse at me depending on the circumstances. Some are well—kept and others smell like a combination of someone that hasn't showered in a year, moth balls, piss, and vomit. In Korea, the old women walk in packs, and God forbid if you're in their way because they will keep walking in the same direction and slam into you. There will be no "excuse me," and they will keep walking. They will stare at you, make disgusted faces, spit in front of you or on you, elbow you, and push you. They will cut in front of you in line even if there are 20 people behind you. They really don't care. This is just the way it is, and it is accepted, although not condoned, in Korea. There have been commercials on TV trying to get people to be more aware of their surroundings, but I didn't see any change. I experienced several instances on both sides of this, and I'll tell you about a few.

One time I was outside of the subway, and the girl I was dating at the time kissed me goodbye. An adjumas walking by saw what had transpired, walked up, and hit me. She then slapped my girlfriend and began screaming at her in Korean, calling her a whore, among many other things. There was also a time when an adjumas slammed into me on the street. By doing so, she apparently hurt herself and began to yell at me and cause a scene. A Korean gentleman who spoke English walked over and asked her first what happened. She told him I assaulted her and that she wanted the police. He asked me what happened, and I told him I was just walking and she slammed into me. It went back and forth for a while, until the cops came and I explained what happened. The police understood and let me go, but it still wasted an hour of my time.

I also one time had an adjumas spit on me while waiting for the bus. I was quite pissed off and screamed at her in Korean. She had no idea what I was talking about and ignored what she had done. A young Korean girl behind her pulled out a napkin and wiped off my pants. She then told the woman that she was rude and should apologize. The woman proceeded to just say I was a foreigner and got on the bus.

But I've also had some great experiences with adjumas. I've had some wonderful conversations and many who were genuinely interested in me and what I was doing in Korea. They're not all bad, but I definitely had more bad experiences than good ones. There are a lot of intolerant people out there. People are ignorant wherever you go. The trick is to try to not let it bother you.

Adjushis are similar to adjumas but different in some ways as well. In general, in Korea you will deal with adjushis more on a daily basis because they are everywhere. Every cab, bus, and train you take has an adjushi driver. They also drive their motorcycles everywhere like crazy suicidal maniacs without a care in the world about anything in front of them. They are similar to adjumas in the sense that they will push, shove you, spit in front of you, or slam into you all the time. They, however, usually understand a little English and sometime will say sorry if you say something to them. I found it easier to deal with adjushis because I had to talk with them more often. One thing that is drastically different is that from 3 to 8 p.m., there are so many adjushis out on the street drunk from drinking Soju after work. They also pass out everywhere in random places. There is a website dedicated to this, called Blackout Korea, and it has some hilarious photos of people passed out all over the place. It also has pictures of foreigners as well, so don't be surprised if you've been there and see yourself on the site.

All in all in most cases, you will probably find adjumas and adjushis to be rude and disrespectful. In a lot of cases, they just don't know any better, or they don't care. You get used to it after a while, but it still doesn't make it right.

CHAPTER ELEVEN

Learning the Language

What does it truly take to learn a language? Well, it doesn't take a brain scientist to tell you that the older you get, the harder it is. I have two nephews and one niece that are being raised bilingual because their parents come from different countries and speak several different languages between them. They are doing it the smart way, as I would if I were in their position. One parent speaks in one language, while the other speaks to them in another. This is effective for them to learn both languages equally. I wish I had that growing up. I wish I was completely bilingual. Unfortunately I'm not, but I've learned a few things along the way on how to learn and do it so that you remember what you learned.

Upon entering Korea, I knew nothing of the language, just how to say hello. Anyounghaseo! You can easily pick up the basics of "hello," "goodbye," and "How much is it?" But, if you really want to learn, it will take studying and some hard work. I didn't do it the right way, but in my opinion I figured out the best way to do it by talking to people who learned quicker and faster than I did. So, here goes.

The first thing you need to do is learn the alphabet. It will seriously take you no more than an hour to do so with a little practice to follow. Get a set of flash cards, write out the letters, and have someone say the sounds to you. With the exception of a few like 의 (uh-ee while gritting your teeth), they are very easy to pronounce. Once you know the alphabet, you can read everything you see. It's that easy.

The next step is to get a private tutor. If you can afford to pay for one, then do it, or offer a language exchange. By doing a language exchange, you'll get lessons for free and only have to help someone with his or her conversation skills. The best book to get to learn Korean is published by Sogang University KLEC and costs about 30,000 KRW or $25 USD. The book is updated very often, and it gets better every time. Have your tutor bring you through it, and by the end, you will end up speaking beginner level conversation. You'll know numbers, money, how to tell time, and how to get around, as well as be able to talk to people for a few minutes, order food, and answer the basic questions you're asked every day.

If you want to learn more Korean, there are several classes offered all over the place. I would take a university course if you can, but for me, due to my schedule, I never had the time. I still learned a lot over the three years I was there and could talk to most people for at least a few minutes or more. Taxi drivers are the best to practice with and were my favorite conversations to have. Overall it's a matter of how much you need and want to learn, depending on how long you will be there and the nature of your time there. You really only need to learn the basics if you're a teacher. The students aren't allowed to speak Korean in class. It can help you, though. Because I spoke intermediate Korean, I could understand what the kids were saying most of the time, and it helped me help them. In business, the more you know, the better.

I tried several other resources that were available in Korea, and let me warn you or guide you away from certain places. The first one is going to a hagwon. Don't do this. Number one, it will cost you a fortune, and two, the people there are not trained to teach you Korean. There are a few exceptions, but they also cost even more money. Going to the free classes offered is a good idea for practice, but every place I went to I found to be very congested with people only half interested in learning. People talked rather than listened and were more interested in meeting girls or guys. I also took classes at the church that I went to. These classes were OK, but usually seemed too fast, and it involved a lot of self—learning. I felt like I needed a tutor to keep up with the pace of the class. It was also held in a gym area where several classes were taking place at once. There was so much exterior or white noise it was hard to concentrate the majority of the time. Looking back, although I stuck it out for nine months, I would have been better just hiring with a private tutor.

One method that you will hear all the time is to get a Korean girlfriend or boyfriend. This is bullocks. Don't believe this. Number one, the person will have to speak far better English than you for you to learn Korean from her or him. Second, you always get sidetracked, if you know what I mean. It's better for you to remained focused on your goal than complicate a relationship with learning a language. Even so, if you are learning, you can practice conversation with them casually. Don't be surprised if they laugh at you, though. Korean people generally don't understand that it's insulting if they laugh at you when you are trying. If anything, they should try to help you, but they usually don't.

So, what you want to do is this. Ask yourself the question, "Why do I want to learn the language?" When you know the answer, you'll know how much you need to learn. If you're just learning it so you can try to pick people up at the local clubs, don't waste your time. You'll be turned away like the thousands of people before you that have tried the same thing.

Backwards Korea: Illogical Thinking and Behavior

Each and every one of us is born somewhere, and how we grow up is determined by that. The culture from there and what we learn to be true and real is typically all that we know. When you go and live abroad, a part of this is stripped from you. It happens slowly, but eventually the wool is pulled off your eyes and you begin to see the world as it truly is.

Ever hear the phrase, "Why do you have to make things so difficult?" If you have, then this chapter will definitely open your mind up to the Korean concept of thinking. I don't think anyone can fully describe the levity that this carries in Korea. The Korea people just do things differently. This is actually true about most cultures in different countries. The trick to it is to understand that this is really just a culture difference. But even though this is just a culture difference, it will be one of the things that annoy you the most.

What's the better way? Build a bridge first that causes a traffic jam every day, so there is no more traffic. Or, build a three-story Dunkin' Donuts in one week. I found that the answer to this riddle was easy. If it is something where you will spend your money, it will be done in a few days. If it is something that will be an inconvenience to you, it will take forever.

Another good example was tearing up and re-doing the sidewalks in the winter. I'm not a construction site worker, but even I know concrete doesn't work so well in the cold. Not just one side at a time either—both sides at the same time so everyone was walking in the street, which caused major traffic problems for a year.

One of my favorites to complain about was how people walked in Korea. Everybody seems to walk very slowly and in a line. It's like a wall coming towards you, and you basically have to slam through it to get by. This is even worse when it rains because you're likely to be stabbed by several umbrellas at any given time.

The largest and perhaps most complained about cultural difference by foreigners was the lack of compliance with actual laws in Korea. I could never understand this. The people just don't comply with the laws, and the police do not enforce the laws. What I mean by this is that there are several laws in Korea that should be practiced, but aren't. One of these is traffic laws. People drive motorcycles at high speeds down a busy sidewalk. You have to jump out of the way or you'll get hit. People driving on the road are crazy, most especially taxi drivers, and I swore several times that the purpose of a traffic light must have been a joke. They stop on green, speed through yellow, and when they see red, they hit the gas like they're in a high-speed chase. I was hit by a car in Korea. I was actually walking down a pedestrian street where cars are not supposed to drive. I stopped and was talking on my phone trying to get directions, and this dumb Korean girl hit me. She said, "Why are you standing on the walkway?" I said, "Because this is where people walk." She said, "I'm sorry, I didn't see you." I told her she was an idiot for driving down a walkway full of pedestrians. I ended up going to the hospital and getting my knee X-rayed and luckily only ended up with a sprain. The good news was that insurance companies in Korea will just pay you off, and I was paid 2,000,000 KRW to basically go away. That's about $1,800 USD to you and me. I was OK with that because I was barely injured.

You will find that no matter where you travel, people will do things differently than you do, and some things will seem completely illogical, but it's just their culture. Try not to fault them for it, but you can feel free to laugh about it later.

CHAPTER THIRTEEN

Korean Tourism

Boryeong Mud Festival in Korea, is perhaps
the most famous amongst foreigners

Ask a Korean person what the best country is to visit and they will probably say Korea. I lived there a long time, and I traveled to several countries in Asia to know this is not true. The problem has more to do with Korea's idea of tourism and its culture towards foreigners. There are lots of wonderful and beautiful places to see in Korea, but they are not geared towards foreigners and tourism.

Here's an example. When I was in Thailand, from the airport to everywhere I went, everyone was friendly. Ask someone for directions, no problem. This won't happen in Korea. Maybe if you ask a foreigner, but don't plan on it. It is very common for two things to happen when asking natives for directions in Korea. The first is that they will help you, but not know which direction to send you, so they'll just point in the wrong direction. This, I think, coincides with the save-face part of their culture. By save-face, I mean that they do not like to be in a situation where they don't know what to say or do. They always try to present in the positive. The other situation is that they'll plow you over like you don't exist. These people are just rude.

Korea for a long time has been trying to increase its tourism. The problem is it's too far behind other countries that are already doing it right. Some examples would be places like Thailand or the Philippines. Also, the Korean culture has a split view about foreigners in its country. Some Koreans will love you and others will hate you. There are a lot of stereotypes that are thrown around about foreigners—mainly, that foreigners are drug users, rapists, and party animals. This is true in many countries, but in my opinion, it was the worst in Korea. Korea has a bad reputation in regards to racism, and a lot of foreigners I knew living there couldn't tolerate it. I'm not big on racism and stereotypes, and I hate when people use them. I stuck it out regardless, though, mainly because of the great friends I had made.

The last year that I was there I tried to visit several different locations in Korea, because I wanted to make sure I saw everything I could. There are still several places I never got the chance to see, but I saw most of them. In no particular order, these are some of the places in Seoul and outside of Seoul that I found to be great places to visit.

In Seoul, there are several places that are worth checking out. One of my favorites was the Seoul Tower. Its official name is the CJ Seoul Tower, but it is commonly known as Namsan Tower or Seoul Tower. This tower was built to mark the highest point in Seoul and stands at 1,574 feet. It's used as a communication and observation tower. The sights you can view from the top are amazing. You can almost see from one side of the peninsula to another on a clear day.

My second favorite was Gyeongbokgung Palace, which was not far from where I lived in Dongdaemun, Seoul. To you and me, it might look very similar to a park. It has beautiful grounds and was the one place in Seoul I could take my shoes off and actually step on the grass. It only cost 1,000 KRW, or 75 cents, to get in. I spent several days off here reading, writing, and relaxing. The palace and grounds consist of official quarters, living quarters and resting places. There are several palaces throughout Korea, and they are all quite beautiful, but this was my favorite place to relax.

Without question, my favorite streets to walk down were in Insadong, Seoul. The streets are filled with shops and thrift stores selling antiques, old books, paintings, and ceramics, as well as several art galleries and exhibit halls. You can also find many traditional tea houses, ethnic restaurants, and traditional shops here.

If you love shopping, Dongdaemun Fashion Town, Namdaemun Market, and Myeong-dong are absolutely the best places I've ever shopped. They do offer tours if you want, but I would say it's better just to take a day and walk through them. You can find anything you want at half the normal price—even less if you know how to haggle. Try this phrase: "Ka ka jew say yo." It means, "Give me a discount." In Dongdaemun, you can also find the upscale fashion shopping malls such as Doota and Migliore.

Namdaemun Market is another great place to shop. Namdaemun literally sells everything! You can always find what you're looking for as long as you have enough time to find it. But if you don't like crowds, I would suggest staying away from both these shopping areas. Approximately 500,000 people go there every day.

Myeong-dong, which has been rated the number-one destination visited by foreign tourists, is crowded with people all year round. Too many people for my taste, but there are a lot of great foreign clothing stores here from many countries around the world. If you're into fashion, this is definitely where you should be shopping, but be prepared to pay for it.

Another great place to visit is the DMZ just north of Seoul. The DMZ is where you can see the truce line that separates Korea into south and north, making it the only divided country in the world. Public access to the DMZ is strictly restricted, and the area is guarded by both South and North Korean soldiers, so don't try to jump the fence. There are several observatories as well, and you might even get a glimpse of North Korean residents through one of the telescopes.

Perhaps one of the most popular places to visit in Korea is Jeju-do Island. Jeju is Korea's southernmost island and was formed by volcanic activity. It looks much like the Hawaiian Islands in the summer. There are several tours, but I recommend the Geomun Oreum lava caves where you can see lava pillars and traces of where lava once flowed. You should also go to Seongsan Ilchulbong Peak (Sunrise Peak) to watch the magnificent view of the sun rising over the sea cliffs at dawn. It was breathtaking and probably the best sunrise I've ever seen.

I also took a trip to Busan with a group of Toastmasters my second year in Korea and really loved the area. It was just before the summer got into full gear, so it wasn't that hot. Summer in Korea can be brutal with the humidity, so I was visiting at the right time. Busan is a beautiful port city located near the southern tip of the Korean peninsula and is surrounded on three sides by ocean. It therefore has several beaches, including Haeundae Beach, which is the most popular. Busan has lots of bars and restaurants and is particularly busy during the summer vacation season.

You should also visit Haedong Yonggungsa Temple in Busan. It features picturesque scenery as it towers over the ocean, plus it has a dragon-shaped stone sculpture, Korea's largest Buddha statue, and a wishing rock.

If you like to climb mountains or ski, Korea is definitely the place for you. Virtually the entire peninsula is one big mountain. If you can handle it, Seoraksan Mountain, Jirisan Mountain and Geumgangsan Mountain offer the pleasure of a beautiful nature experience, but they are very steep. Seoraksan Mountain has a number of peaks and valleys, including Korea's third-highest peak.

Jirisan Mountain is Korea's first national park. Though it is famous for its steep and towering peaks, it is also good for family and novice climbers as there are various paths on the mountain.

If you're an avid skier, you have to check out Gangwon-do in the winter. Gangwon-do's ski resorts offer diverse slopes and various facilities. Yongpyeong Resort is huge and has 31 different slopes of all difficulties. There is also Daemyung Vivaldi Park, which is close to Seoul, but often packed with people and impossible to actually ski. It does also have an indoor water park called Ocean World, located underground beneath the resort.

Sometimes in life we all need to take a break and find peace within our own right. Korea has several Buddhist temples in Korea that you can visit. I'm not Buddhist, but I found it to be a great way to clear my head and get away from the hustle of everyday life. Korea's Buddhist temples are located deep within mountains and are in perfect harmony with the surrounding nature. There are three major Buddhist temples in Korea. The first is Haeinsa Temple, located at Gaya Mountain. The second is Tongdosa Temple, which is famous for not having any Buddhist statues in the temple. The third is Songgwangsa Temple, which means "a rest area for clouds and winds."

I'm sure there are many other great places in Korea, but those are the ones I went to. I have always enjoyed learning about history and the culture of different civilizations, and it was a real treat to be able to learn so much firsthand about a country different from my own.

CHAPTER FOURTEEN

The End of an Era:
Leaving Korea

CZ, Me, Jason, and Robyn at my birthday party in Itaewan 2009.

After more than two and a half years teaching in Korea, I returned home in December of 2009 to visit my family for the holidays. It was a great vacation, and I was happy to see all my friends and family that I had missed so dearly while I was away. I had already secured a job at a new school called

English Friends in Korea and planned to start after I returned from the U.S. in January.

At the time I was in a serious relationship and had a great, beautiful Korean girlfriend, Eunmi, whom I loved. I really thought my life was finally heading in the right direction. I also had the best friends I could ask for while living abroad. I loved my life at the time. How could I have gone wrong? I even had an awesome apartment and a cat that was the best at welcoming me home every day. My job was perfect! Not too demanding, but it challenged me enough that I liked it, and my students generally wanted to learn English. My schedule was even very good. Not to mention that my Toastmasters Club had elected me president, and we were doing great things spreading better public speaking throughout Korea.

I'm a planner, and I like to know what I have in store for me, or I at least plan ahead of time in my mind what my future will be and look like. I thought I was going to be in Korea the rest of my life. I was very wrong about this, but how could I have known what was about to transpire?

After returning to Korea from the U.S., my awesome friend Sam picked me up at the airport. It was great to see him, and I realized at this point how good I really had it. Some of the friendships I developed while I was living abroad really did rival that of some of my relationships in the U.S. Here I was once again about to embark upon a new journey that I had planned out so meticulously. I was about to have everything that I could possibly want. I had my friend Sam drop me off in Itaewan so I could see my beautiful girlfriend. It was wonderful to see her after a month, and we exchanged gifts and caught up.

The next month went on seemingly as planned. I got my apartment set up and began working at my new school. I technically shouldn't have been working, but sometimes in Korea your employer will allow you to while you wait for your visa. It was a couple weeks later that I got the worst news possible. It was a Tuesday mid-afternoon, and my school manager asked me to come back to the school so he could talk to me. After arriving, he sat me down and told me my visa had been denied. I didn't really understand. I had been working in Korea for the last two and a half years and nothing had changed. I submitted all the same paperwork, but this time I was denied because I had a dismissed misdemeanor on my record. Even my school manager couldn't believe it. Korea at the time was trying to make it harder to get a visa and raise its teaching standards. I was on the receiving end of these new standards and was denied my E2 (teaching) visa.

I can't describe in words what I felt at that moment in time. I can only say that I was completely devastated and knew that everything was going to change. I did some investigating and appealed the decision, but was once again told I couldn't teach under an E2 visa anymore. What was I to do? I was so happy before and things were going so well. I had plans for the future, and now none of it was going to work out. I started by telling my girlfriend, who was devastated, to say the least. We talked about what the possibilities were and how we could make things work, but I knew I was going to have to leave Korea. I also knew that once I left, everything I had held so dear would change, and I would once again be embarking on a new journey.

I took the next step right away by putting my résumé online and started looking for jobs in other countries in Asia. I had many options, but Thailand, Taiwan, and China looked the most promising. Due to timing and paperwork issues, it was China that worked out and I was offered a job working for EF English First. It was known as a good company with a good track record, so I took the job. There was one huge problem: The job didn't start until April. What was I going to do for two months? Thankfully some things worked out in my favor. I was allowed to stay in my apartment as long as I paid the rent, and I found some part-time tutoring work. A week later, my old co-teacher Iny from my first hagwon called me and told me that there was an emergency teacher position open at my old school. This was due to two teachers pulling the midnight run. This is when you get your paycheck and fly out the same day. The school desperately needed a teacher, and I was able to work there through the end of March. The school also gave me a place to live and paid me well under the circumstances. I can't say I was eager to work there again after all they put me through, but I really didn't have a choice.

For the next two months, I did my best to tie things up. Eunmi and I stayed together, although things weren't really the same. I continued with everything I had been doing, but started telling everyone I was leaving. I spent as much time with my friends as possible and said goodbye to those I knew I would most likely never see again. Two months flew by relatively quickly. Before I knew it, my flight was a week away. I had a goodbye party that was awesome, and all my friends from around Seoul came to give me a great send-off. It was bittersweet. I was so sad to leave everything I had known for almost three years, but in some ways had come to terms with it all. Some of my greatest friends and people I looked up to in Korea had told me that life has a way of working itself out. I was a little excited about going to China. After all, it was on the top of my list of places to visit in Asia that I had yet to go to. So the last night before I left, my friends and I partied it up until the late hours of the morning. I crashed at my buddy's house and woke up in the morning to catch my bus to the airport. The whole way I was staring out the window, thinking about everything that had transpired and changed over the years. My only interruption was a phone call to say my last goodbyes to Eunmi. Off to China I was going, and a new adventure and journey I was about to embark on.

Welcome to Shanghai

Getting to Shanghai wasn't as easy as I would have liked to thought. Imagine carrying around two big suitcases bound together, an Army-size enormous duffel bag, and a backpack loaded with crap. Yup, I was that guy. I had even shipped two boxes to China so that I had less to carry. I guess I should have sent a few more boxes.

Before getting to Shanghai, I had to stop over in Hong Kong to get my visa. It was a process like anything, but I had been to Hong Kong a few times already and knew the city well enough to get around, and thankfully most people spoke English.

Upon arriving, I took a taxi to my hotel. Who would've thought that I was going to have to drag my baggage a couple of blocks to get there? My cab driver was nice enough to drop me off in the wrong spot. Not fun trying to drag my bags through the hundreds of people on the street, but I made it. After dropping off my luggage, I was able to take a quick shower and head off to the embassy. There was, of course, a long line when I arrived, but I got in, filled out my paperwork, and had to return the next day to pick up my visa.

That night I went out the Soho and Lao Kwai Fong. This is the part of the city with all the clubs and nightlife. I walked around and eventually found a cool bar to hang out in. I ended up meeting a group of people on vacation and hung out with them until early morning and then went back to my hotel.

Later that morning I woke up and went back to the embassy. To my surprise, there was no line this time, but when I went to pick up my visa I was denied. I can only say that my face had "what the fuck" written all over it. I had the number to my recruiter in Shanghai and called her from a pay phone. She told me to apply for a tourist visa to enter mainland China and that I would have to go back to Hong Kong, but it would be paid for by EF. I lucked out there! A free all-expense paid trip to Hong Kong is awesome! She assured me it wasn't a problem, but my flight was the next day at noon. I didn't think the visa would process in time. Anyway, I filed the paperwork and asked that they rush it. They told me they couldn't, but I said I would come back to pick it up tomorrow. And so that night I went to watch a movie in 3D, and then went to bed early. I woke up at 8 a.m. and headed off to the embassy. After waiting in line for an hour, I went to try and pick up my visa. The receptionist told me to come back at 2 p.m. I told her my flight was at noon and I couldn't miss it. Luckily for me she was nice and went to look for my visa. She returned a few minutes later and said, "OK, you're all set. Please pay next window." I was about to go ballistic, but then just smiled in disbelief. And there you have it: I had my visa and was off to Shanghai.

I took a taxi back to my hotel, asked the driver wait, grabbed my luggage and had him take me to the airport. I got there just in time for my three-hour flight and off I went. I slept the whole plane ride up until right before we landed. I didn't get a chance to see the city from the plane, but I could tell from what little I saw that it was very big. Nothing like flying out of Boston. The second you leave Boston, you can see the edge of the city. This city went on forever.

Once I landed, customs was usual—a long line that you eventually get through, but otherwise not a problem. Thankfully, unlike my arrival to Korea, there was actually someone waiting for me this time. I can tell you, though, that it wouldn't have surprised me if no one was there. It was a little while before we were able to leave. We had to wait for another two teachers to arrive before driving into the city. Once they got there, we drove into the city and to a wonderful hotel called The Longemont Hotel. The ride wasn't that long, and it was cool to see a new city I had never been to before. The hotel was beautiful, and I couldn't believe that was where I was staying. Well, that's because I was really staying next door at a smaller unknown hotel that no one knew the name of. It was, however, really nice inside and would be my home for the next two weeks while I went through orientation and found a place to live.

Unlike Korea, schools in China don't offer you housing. Instead they give you a housing stipend and you find your own housing close to the school you work at. The next two weeks went by pretty fast, and my adventure in China was just beginning.

CHAPTER SIXTEEN

EF English First

EF English First Co-teachers and Staff on a
field trip to Happy Valley in Shanghai

EF Education First, usually just called EF, was the company
I was hired by to teach in Shanghai. EF is an international
education company that specializes in language training. It has
400-plus schools, in more than 50 countries worldwide, and is
the largest privately held education provider in the world.

The actual part of the company I worked for was EF English First. That is the division that provides English-language training. EF English First provides English training services for adults and children in China, Indonesia, and Russia.

I'll start off by saying that with the exception of the director of my academy branch, EF treated me extremely well. My director, on the other hand, was a complete asshole. You'll understand why I say that later and agree with me for sure.

Unlike hagwons in Korea, EF truly has a decent program and is, for the most part, well organized. The company is on top of its game when it comes to screening staff and making sure that all your paperwork is taken care of. Those kinds of things always scared me in Korea, and even before going to Hong Kong for my visa, but EF took care of it. I never had any problems when it came to my visa, taking vacations, or anything really. In Korea, it seemed like there was always some problem caused by something wrong on my paperwork, and it would cost me hundreds of dollars to fix.

If you remember all that horrible stuff I talked about several chapters back in regards to Korean hagwons, this is not the case with EF. For one, you'll actually be trained for about three weeks or until you feel you're ready. The company will also will start you off slow usually and gradually add the number of classes that you teach until you have a full schedule. I really lucked out and didn't have a full schedule for the first two months. Another thing that I liked, perhaps loved about EF, was that the students evolved from the program. What I mean is that the program was designed in a step-by-step process, and the students had to learn one step after another. In Korea, it was very common to have a variety of students in your class with very different English speaking proficiency. Another great thing was that you would end up teaching the same lesson more than once. I saved all my work, so when I had to teach a new class the same lesson, it was already done.

A few things did bother me, but I think a lot of it had to do with my director of studies and the Chinese culture. The first was the favoritism given to the Chinese staff. Sometimes I felt like they could kill someone and get away with it. Another problem I had was the last-minute changing of the schedule and poor planning by the director. If I was lucky, I had a lesson already prepared, but sometime I was forced to just wing it.

In general, though, it was a good to school to work for and much better and easier than working for a hagwon in Korea. I do have to give great thanks to my lead teacher, Sam Evans, who not only gave me many lessons that I was able to use in my classes, but also for being an awesome friend. He was always there to help, and I really appreciated it.

CHAPTER SEVENTEEN

Culture Shock Once Again

It goes without saying that no matter what country you go to, you'll be in for at least some kind of culture shock. This time I think it took a while for it to kick in. At first glance I didn't see that much of a difference between Shanghai and Seoul, other than the fact that there was considerably more smog, and it was visibly much dirtier. Shanghai, being a megacity, is hard to come to terms with in regards to size. It is absolutely huge—2,448 square miles, to be exact. To give you an idea of comparison, New York City is only 469 square miles. The amount of people, cars, motorcycles, taxis, and bicycles in Shanghai truly is astounding. If that doesn't surprise you, this might: Shanghai also has and is building more skyscrapers than any other city in the world at this time. The night skyline truly is amazing.

It was a few weeks later after beginning to settle in that I started to feel the shock of being in a new city. My first couple of weeks had consisted of training for my new school, EF English First, finding an apartment and getting orientated to my surroundings. I very easily became friends with my lead teacher, Sam Evans, a tall, lanky chap from Nottingham,

England. Minus the fact that he was an Englishman, he was great at making me feel welcome, showing me the ropes, and taking me out for a pint or two in the big city. Once I got my bearings, it was little things like seeing people pissing on the sides of the streets everywhere that I found very unappealing. I'm not sure what the social norm is in China, but from what I gather, it's a combination of the very rich, the very poor, and the in-between morphing together to form some strange paradox. The very rich people in China seem to be well-kept, have manners, and do things as I would call it normally. But then you see people bathing in the streets, grandparents holding their grandchildren over trash cans to take a shit, and people spitting all over the place. I think it's allowed and tolerated because there are so many non-educated people in China, but I don't think that's a good enough excuse. It just makes you feel like everything is very dirty. I can tell you I almost washed the skin off my hands for the first month trying to avoid catching the plague.

Once you get used to it, I guess it's not all that bad. Some things were very similar to Korea, like the crazy taxi drivers and motorcycles driving all over the sidewalks and roadways like no one else is around. The subway in Shanghai was also a sardine packing machine just like Seoul in the fact that everybody pushes and shoves to get in and out. Traveling at peak hours on the subway was definitely something I wanted to avoid.

I think the main thing that I noticed was that it was very difficult to find someone who spoke English in Shanghai, and far less people spoke English in China than I thought. What I found out was that the same amount of people speak English in China as in Seoul, but the difference is that China is so big compared to Korea, and those people are spread out across the country. In Seoul you can walk around easily speaking English and get by. This is not true in China at all. If you can't speak the basic lingo, you're pretty much screwed. I started taking classes and studying right away. I'm a true believer that if you go to another country and don't learn the language, you are ignorant and limiting your potential. The main problem with this is that Chinese has to be the most difficult language to learn. The word "mao" has about 1,000 different meanings depending on the tone and placement of the word. How was I going to learn? Classes and practice, and even now, after being there almost a year, all I can do is say a few phrases, get a taxi, and order food. It was over the next several months that I read, observed, practiced, and adjusted to the many other customs and traditions in Shanghai. It was Gaungxi that I learned was most important.

CHAPTER EIGHTEEN

Gaungxi:
"What the Hell Does That Mean?"

In China, building personal relationships is everything because people will not trust you on face value. Word of mouth weighs very heavily in the minds of the Chinese. I've always been a very sociable person, but I truly found it difficult at first to build any kind of bond with the local people. Part of this problem was that I couldn't speak Chinese, and learning the language was and is extremely difficult. It was "Gaungxi" that I didn't understand and that I didn't have. There is no real definition for "Gaungxi," but I'll do my best to explain it. In layman's terms, this means personal connected relationships, but it goes way beyond that.

After a couple of months in Shanghai, I decided I needed to branch out and get involved with something outside of work. In Korea, I was involved in several different Toastmaster clubs, and I made lots of friends and business contacts this way. I tried going to a few Toastmaster meetings in Shanghai, but it just wasn't the same. The main problem I had with it was the format of their meetings and that they weren't following the Toastmaster rules and guidelines. The clubs I was a part of in

Korea were very prestigious, and would never let that kind of thing happen. The other problem was that it didn't jive with my work schedule.

One of my friends from Seoul put me in contact with George Felbinger. George was the Chicago China Club founder and sourcing consultant and had 18 years of China business experience in Shanghai. The Chicago China Club was created to establish connections for people who were looking to do business in either Chicago or China, but mainly was about bringing like-minded people from all cultures and backgrounds together. I sent George an e-mail, and he invited me to one of his functions. To my surprise, it was through meeting people at this event that I began to find those personal connections I was looking for. George was great at making me feel welcome, and I would continue going to these monthly events for the rest of my time in China.

At each event that I went to, I continued to meet businessmen and women who were doing great things, not only in business but also entrepreneurial ventures. It was through talking to these people and reconnecting with them again over coffee or at other functions that I learned that building personal connections in China meant everything. Several people I became closer with led me to ways to make extra money by tutoring or consulting. These people took me to parties and networking events all over the city. They ranged from small venues and hole-in-the-wall bars I could never find on my own to five-star luxury hotels. I was chauffeured around the city and treated like a rock star for the most part. It wasn't all fun and games, though. Some people I did small favors for, like editing a document, and with others I traded services. I once taught a class for free just to get introduced to the right person. I ended up being taken advantage of once or twice, but it was all worth it because it was "Gaungxi" that I had gained. Think of it this way: When you go for a job interview, you have to give references. Or, if you're trying to do business with a new company, it wants to know that you have a proven track record. In China, if you have "Gaungxi," none of this matters. Chinese people are extremely loyal for the most part. If you form strong relationships with them, they will do anything for you. These relationships will last forever if you want them to. I still keep in contact with several people I met in China, and they continue to be great people to talk with. If you ever go to China for business or an extended stay, do you best to extend your hand of friendship. Be sincere, and not only will you further yourself in your business dealing, but you'll also meet some wonderful people and greatly enhance your life while being abroad.

CHAPTER NINETEEN

Name Cards

Just like in Korea, having a business card, or name card as they call it in Asia, is very important in China. I would say it's even more important in China than in Korea. Without a name card, you have no credibility. In Korea, however, it's not as much expected. Upon the first instance of meeting a person in China, he or she will present you with a business card and expect you to do the same. This is a way of introduction, or a way of sizing you up so that he may know a little more about you and what you may be able to do help him, or what he might be able to do to help you.

Chinese people follow this rule in explicit fashion. Trying to meet a Chinese businessman without a name card would be as hard as trying to find a desert without sand. Executives, secretaries, professors, ESL teachers, and cab drivers alike all have business cards. Even some of my students from my school had business cards. It's a weird custom I think to foreigners to have to have a business card just to introduce yourself, but that's the way it is in China. Meet a fellow teacher and exchange business cards, and sometimes you'll get a good laugh. In China I came across several people with all sorts of cards, ranging from a practically blank card with just a name and number, to cards that were very elaborate and in both languages. Teachers had the best ones. My favorite was this teacher Peter whose business card said, "Professional Basket Weaver." If you don't get the joke, well, let's just say that as long as you got a degree from an accredited college, even in basket weaving, you can get a job teaching abroad in Asia.

Having a name card in China is imperative, but what it says is very important. After reading your name, people will look at your title and instantly categorize who you are in the grand scheme of their own lives. But more than that, they have to be able to read it first. More so in China than any other country I visited in my four years living abroad, the language barrier in China is quite prevalent, probably because of the mass numbers of people. You can't just walk the street and try to talk to people. Most will have no idea what you're saying. This is why having your name card both in Chinese and English is very important. English is the unofficial second language of China. If you think it will be expensive to print name cards, well, not really. You could have your card translated and printed in China for 40 RMB for three hundred cards. That's roughly $6 USD. Pretty cheap considering the business cards I just printed for my current job cost twenty bucks for one hundred.

I learned a lot after reading my friend's book, "A Focused Pursuit in China," in which he talks about the importance of name cards. Having a business card in China is only the first part. It goes hand and hand with the whole "Guangxi" thing. It's not like the U.S. or other countries. In the U.S, I don't hand my card over to everybody I meet. If I feel it's necessary, or that they might be in need of my services, then sure, why not. I'm not going to hand it some random guy I meet at the coffee shop. You also usually hand someone a business card at the end of your conversation in the U.S. But in China, when and how you present and receive a name card is also important. You must present the card facing the person you are giving it to and have the card and letters facing them. You must present the card holding it with both hands, and with both thumbs and index fingers. You must receive a card the same way. After receiving a card, you actually have to take the time to read what it says. To not do this is considered an insult in Chinese culture and implies that you consider the person of no value. I found that asking the person a question and/or giving a compliment really went a long way, even if my words were not fully understood. If it's someone you can have a conversation with, relish it, and try to learn something, and maybe you could end up doing business together.

Asian Subway Systems

The Seoul Metropolitan Subway is located primarily in Seoul and is the world's second most highly used rapid transit system after the Tokyo Subway. It has 18 different lines and expands to nearby Incheon, where the airport is, and other satellite cities just outside Seoul. Seoul Subway is considered the world's best subway. This is because of its cleanliness, ease of use, accurate arrival times, and innovations such as the world's longest circular line and completely driverless lines. Seoul Subway also is unique in having all stations installed with automatic platform gates for safety. Another great feature is that all directional signs in the system are written in both Korean and English, and there is a pre-recorded voice announcement that says the station name in Korean followed by English.

Those were all the good things you will hear about the Korean subway. What you won't hear is how packed it is, especially during rush hour from 6 to 9 a.m. and 4:30 to 6:30 p.m. The people are typically extremely rude and will push, shove, step on you, and sometimes even punch you to get where they need to go. Picture five people stuffed inside a phone booth. That's about what you can expect to see on the subway.

Although the subway is cleaned regularly, several people have terrible hygiene in Korea, and standing next to them is like sticking your head in a sewage tank. Certain subway lines like the green and brown constantly smell like puke and urine because they are lines used to get to the party districts of Hongdae and Itaewan. I also can't forget to mention the sleeping commuters. It's like no one sleeps at night, and only in the subway. Don't be surprised if someone's head ends up in your lap. And, occasionally some subway stations are shut down without notice, so you may just happen to get off at the wrong station if you're not paying attention. Otherwise, it was a great way to get from one side of the city to another, and despite its downsides, I used it regularly.

The Shanghai Metro is very similar to the subway system in Seoul, but much larger. In fact, it is the longest network in the world, spanning more than 270 miles. There are currently 11 different metro lines, and the system continues to grow, with new lines and extensions of old lines currently under construction. Shanghai is much bigger than Seoul, and you can expect the same kind of business as in Korea. Unlike Korea's subway, Shanghai's is not as clean and does not have gates at every station to protect the riders. Due to constant construction, you could also have to walk up to a mile to transfer from one train to another. It can be very inconvenient, especially during inclement weather.

Japan has the world's largest supreme train network. Nearly half of all commuters travel by train in Tokyo. Once again, much like Seoul and Shanghai, the Tokyo subway has serious issues with the amount of people trying to ride at any given time. During peak rush hour, it is really unbelievable. It literally looks like a stampede of cattle being forced into a corral.

You're squished together so tightly, you can't even breathe. But, one thing that is different about the subways in Japan is the rude, pushy staff. You know the saying that you can't fit ten pounds of shit in a five-pound bag? Well, they'll beg to differ in Japan, and that's exactly what the staff does. They actually are called pushers, too. And just like Seoul, commuters in Tokyo can often be found sleeping or passed out in the subway, usually because of drinking the night before or their three-hour commute to work. I also don't suggest trying to catch the last train. It's like it's the last train out of hell, and people go crazy trying to get on it, and the conductors are screaming at everyone on megaphones. If you miss your train, I recommend staying in a capsule hotel as long as you're not claustrophobic. A capsule hotel looks like a large gel capsule you would take for medicine, but you actually sleep in it. It has a small mattress and usually a mini TV. I stayed in one just for the experience, and although really small, it was pretty cool.

There are many other subway systems in Asia, but these are the largest. Be prepared to be pushed, kicked, and stepped on. That's the custom while riding on an Asian subway.

CHAPTER TWENTY-ONE

Eating and Drinking Customs

Socializing around food and mealtimes is very important to the Chinese. Much of Chinese family life revolves around the dinner table. Traditionally, Chinese believed it was impolite to talk too much while eating. A good meal was regarded as too special to be spoiled by conversation. This has changed a little bit now, and conversations are more prevalently held over meals. It is also a common tradition to eat from a common dish in the middle of a round table instead of having food served on individual plates. When sitting at a large round dining table, you are expected to place food on a small plate or on a bowl of rice in front of you. Chinese usually eat from a bowl or small plate. When eating from a bowl, they place spoonfuls of the main dish and sauce on rice in the bowl and bring the bowl close to their mouth and scoop the food into their mouth with chopsticks.

Depending on the customs of the people you're with, this might not take place. They might, however, plunge their chopsticks into a shared dish and eat straight from that. Coming from the U.S. and being a bit of a clean freak, this did weird me out. I felt like I was being infected by everybody I was dining with. Chinese people will also reach across one another when eating, pass dishes, pour each other drinks, and put food on each other's plate. This is, of course, completely opposite of the U.S.A., where is rude to reach over someone's plate.

Chinese food is served in courses. A typical Chinese meal consists of rice, one to four meat or fish main courses, two vegetable dishes, and one soup. The courses are often eaten one at a time. Soup is usually served after the main course instead of before it. Sometimes drinks aren't served. Soup is used to wash down a meal instead of drinks. The Chinese are not big on desserts. Meals are often capped off with fruit—not cake, pies, or ice cream.

Want to be considered crude, rude, or barbaric in China? Try to ask someone to split the bill. Being the one that pays is considered an honor in China. The custom is really quite simple: The person that extends an invitation or the highest ranking person present is the person who pays. You will, however, often see people fighting over the bill. In this case, the most respected individual is expected to win out. If you want to pay the bill in China, be prepared to put up a good fight to pay it. Old-school Chinese never go Dutch.

It also often happens that someone will sneak off to go to the bathroom and take care of the bill so there is no argument. This is because it is considered tacky for the host to pay in front of his guests, so usually he excuses himself under that pretext and pays the bill privately.

If a couple of friends meet by chance on the street and decide to go to a restaurant, usually they will fight with each other over who pays. The "loser" who doesn't pay often suggests going to another place and then pays the bill there.

Chinese usually don't start drinking until someone offers the toast "gam bei" ("dry glass," the equivalent of "bottoms up"). Koreans and Japanese use the same word for their toasts, and it originated in Japan.

The Chinese are very big on toasts. "Gam bei" is heard after every course, and guests are often asked to have one drink with every person who is considered a host. There is Chinese proverb that goes, "If you leave a social meal sober you did not truly enjoy yourself."

A host usually begins the toast after the first course by welcoming all of his guests. Toasts can be offered to the whole table or people sitting around you, and they are usually ushered in with "gam bei." Even though gam bei toasts are offered through the night, you only have to empty your glass on the first one. If you watch this initial toast, the people drain their glasses and show each other the empty glass (ladies are supposed to take only a sip, as it is frowned upon for women to be drunk in public). The Chinese generally don't touch glasses with each other during a toast.

The Chinese often drink shaohsing (red rice wine) when making toasts and beer between toasts. It is not customary for guests to drink only when making or receiving toasts. The first toast is frequently a general one, with everyone drinking together, usually as soon as the first dish is presented. After this it is general practice for all at the table to toast others, starting with host/hostess toasting the guest of honor.

It is not necessary to give a short speech when making a toast, but it is common to specify the kind of toast. The most usual toast is gam bei. Other toasts include sui bian ("drink as you please"), sui yi ("drink a little"), or ban bei ("drink just half the glass"). The whole table often drinks together when new dishes arrive.

It's important to know that when drinking, one should not drink from the bottle. It is also considered impolite to pour a drink for yourself, and when pouring a drink for an older person, you should make sure to use two hands (a sign of respect). If you want a drink yourself, the polite thing to do is fill someone else's glass and he in turn will fill yours. In some situations, it is rude to turn down a drink that is being offered to you. This is especially true at special functions like weddings. To avoid drinking too much, keep your glass full. To avoid being rude, accept a drink the first time it is offered to you by a particular individual. The second time he offers, it is acceptable to politely say no.

Some Chinese are fond of playing the "finger game" (two players fling out numbers on their fingers and make guesses as to how many) with the loser taking a drink. They also play dice games, which consists of bluffing how many of a certain number you have using a combination of everyone's dice.

The Chinese generally do look down on drunkenness. They don't get hammered as much as the Japanese and Koreans. Chinese especially look down on daytime drinking, as people are expected to work and produce for the motherland.

Even though every place I went to was a little different, drinking is a huge part of Asian culture. In every country I visited, it seemed like there were always people out drinking and partying every night of the week. I know in the U.S. you can also go to a bar any night of the week, but in Shanghai and other cities like Seoul, it is a part of their culture. There are several different ways that these customs come in to play. Some are family-oriented, some are for business, and some are for celebration. Knowing about these customs is important. Not only because you could end up drinking to the point that you pass out, but also because it's usually a major insult to refuse a drink if offered.

Sam, my best mate in China and head teacher at EF English First, got married after several months that I was in China. I was asked to sub in for his brother as best man. His brother apparently didn't drink, and I unfortunately didn't understand the ramifications of what this entailed. In China, the best man and the groom are required to have a drink with every member that attended the party. I don't know anyone that can handle drinking 100 or more drinks in a night. Not to mention the fact that they kept offering me cigarettes, too, which you are supposed to smoke with them after the bride lights the cigarettes. I must have puked in the bathroom five times that night in between taking drinks. The worst part was it was that it wasn't just beer, it was also wine. Who chugs wine? I had a lot of fun that night, but I was definitely hung over for several days.

One of the most common places for eating and drinking customs in China is through business meetings. If you think you're going to be able to do a meet-and-greet and settle a business deal in China in one day, you're horribly mistaken. Most business meetings first take place over lunch or dinner with drinks, and business is not discussed, other than maybe talking about what you do in your company. Chinese people like to get you to know you better by seeing you with your guard down and trying to figure out what kind of person you are. They actually want to get to know you more before they do business with you. Unlike the U.S. where everything is strictly business until the deal is done with a possible celebration after, in China it could take several meetings, dinners, and drinking sessions before you get the answer you're so eagerly waiting for. In most cases, the first meeting is a luncheon where you eat, drink, and get to know each other better. The second meeting is where you also will eat and drink, but it's more about business and figuring out if you can help each other and work together. It's the third meeting where the deal is done, and either you part ways or a celebration of your agreement is had.

CHAPTER TWENTY-TWO

Asian Nightlife:
Seoul, Shanghai, Tokyo, and More

Think the nightlife in your city or town is boring? In Korea, every night is Friday night! Perhaps one of the reasons I loved Korea so much was its booming nightlife. Drinking in Korea is a huge part of its culture and is infused with every aspect of life there, or at least it seems that way. Korean businessmen get together practically every day after work and go out to drink soju and makgeolli and congratulate each other on being masters of the universe. The best part of this is when you see them a few hours later passed out on the sidewalk.

Before going to Korea, I had never lived in big city like New York, so maybe my view is a little skewed, but the whole city of Seoul is lit up like a big Christmas tree. It is certainly one of the liveliest cites in the world. Even after midnight, thousands of people wander the streets in all the major shopping districts and popular downtown areas. The top attractions at nighttime are Dongdaemun Market for late-night shopping and the Hongik University (Hongdae) and Itaewan neighborhoods with their high concentration of nightclubs.

If you love having amazing dinners, hearing live music, going to clubs like something out of an Usher or Chris Brown video, and partying like we're all going to die tomorrow, that's the nightlife in Shanghai. It doesn't matter what night of the week it is. Just like Seoul, every night is Friday in Shanghai. This was also true in Seoul, Tokyo, and Bangkok. There are always great deals for food, clubs, and shows no matter what night you choose to go out.

Many locations in Asia are famed for their nightlife, including perennial entertainment favorites such as Tokyo, Singapore, Bangkok, and Macau, which offer virtually any experience under the sun depending on your tastes. Whether you're looking to play casino games, dance into the wee hours at popular clubs, or spend a more refined evening at the ballet or opera, you'll be able to find something to enjoy among the diverse and sprawling continent that is Asia.

Over the last decade, with places like Macau passing Las Vegas as the world's top gambling destination, there are now mega resorts and some of the largest casinos in the world with luxurious hotels and entertainment complexes that include top clubs, bars, and concert venues.

If you are looking for a crazy night in Tokyo, go to Kabuki-cho. Don't go during the day, though, because Kabuki-cho sleeps in the day and comes alive at night.

Tokyo may not offer up any casinos, but it has one of the most vibrant club scenes in all of Asia, with the city's entertainment districts, such as Ginza, Kabuki-cho, and Roppongi, filled to the brim nearly every night. World-famous clubs like AgeHa (which plays host to up to 5,000 clubbers on four different dance floors), Womb, and Club Asia draw visitors from around the globe, with some of the top DJs on the planet dropping in from time to time to show off their stuff in Tokyo.

A lot of people have some idea about what I would consider the craziest city in Asia. If you don't know what city I'm talking about, it's Bangkok. Bangkok's reputation for a louder and rowdier nightlife scene caters to nearly every taste and delight within the sprawling city. Whether you're after a tour of its famed go-go bars, a ladyboy show, gay clubs, or a more sedate night out on a dinner cruise, Bangkok offers it all—and at a fraction of the price that you'll find at many other cities. Bangkok is also an excellent jumping-off point for visitors who go on to explore the rest of Thailand, which offers a wide range of nightlife and entertainment opportunities.

In Asia and especially China, people like to party in one big group rather than breaking up into small groups and circulating like Westerners do at a cocktail party. When Chinese do divide into groups, they make separate groups of men and women. Taking turns singing is a popular activity in Asia, with one person playing the role of "emcee" and calling on the others to participate one by one. If you attend a party like this, it is a good idea to have a song ready in case you are called upon to sing.

You always have to be aware of your surroundings and the kind of place you're in when in Asia. What looks like a normal night club could be a brothel or whorehouse. There was a place just like this with cheap beer that my friends Sam and Craig and I went to in Shanghai. We never could figure out what kind of place it was. We always did have a great time there, though, and after a while, the gentlemen that went there, as well as the owner and bar girls, treated us very well. They would often buy us drinks, and they even sent us business referrals for private students to teach. It might have been a shady place to be, but in some ways it was comfortable, and it was less than a five-minute walk from where we lived.

CHAPTER TWENTY-THREE

Business in Asia

Asia covers China, Japan, Malaysia, Hong Kong, Vietnam, South Korea, The Philippines, and other countries in the Pacific. These countries often have radically distinct cultures with radically distinct etiquette. In this case of Asia, more than any other region, it's best to consult country-specific books for each place you plan to do business. However, I'll share with you what little I learned while I was there. Part of my knowledge about Asian culture came from reading several books like the "Lonely Planet" for each place I traveled to, or others books on culture when I was living in Korea. I made several mistakes along the way like bowing when I wasn't supposed to, or forgetting to bow. It's good to know, though, that in most cases the Asian people are pretty forgiving as long as they see you making an effort to be respectful.

Handshakes, no matter where you go, are a big deal, but Americans routinely mangle Asian handshakes. It's quite simple, actually: When you are in China, Hong Kong, Japan, Indonesia, Malaysia, Singapore, Vietnam, or South Korea, you can shake hands. But avoid direct eye contact during the handshake, and don't shake very hard or very long. It is very possible that your host may bow to you. The more senior you are, the deeper the person will bow. You may also bow. The bow is a sign of mutual respect.

The Philippines is the one exception here. Don't bow, but do make direct eye contact.

Last names and professional titles are used and have great importance across Asia. Don't be afraid to say that you are a professional if you are one.

Meetings begin more or less on time in Japan, China, Hong Kong, South Korea, Thailand, and in the Chinese population of Indonesia, but don't be surprised if they start 15 minutes late. In Malaysia, Vietnam, and the Philippines, meetings are less likely to start punctually.

In China, most of your junior Chinese business associates will arrive early. You do not have to start the meeting ahead of time. They are there in case you need anything.

How you dress is also very important in Asia. Your default business wardrobe for men is conservative business dress, with suits, ties, and tie-up shoes, and for women, conservative suits and dresses. Because of their warmer climates, some leniency in dress is to be found in Vietnam, Malaysia, The Philippines, Singapore, and Hong Kong. But even in these countries, be conservative and avoid flashiness of any kind.

One thing you'll find is that Asians love to entertain their business associates in bars and restaurants and that the food is exquisitely flavored, prepared, and presented.

In China and Hong Kong, expect a banquet. This is a long meal with innumerable courses served one after the other. Arrive on time and get ready to eat. Take something from every serving dish, even if it's only a little amount. But never clean your plate. Symbolically, the magnificence of the meal means that you can't finish it.

In Japan, you will be hosted to an evening of eating and drinking. Let your host order for you and then enjoy something from each platter. Don't refuse to eat sushi or sashimi (both of which involve raw fish) you'll insult your host. I actually had to do this, and it didn't go over well. My host was quite angry with me, and I thought I was going to be asked to leave. Unfortunately, I'm severely allergic to fish, so it took a long time for them to understand that I couldn't eat what they offered me. We basically played a game of charades, and my host finally understood that it could kill me. Once they did, they were sure to order me a separate dish just for me. You should also be careful and make sure you drink your beer or sake slowly because your host will fill your cup every time it's empty.

Koreans entertain both at home and at restaurants. Arrive on time if you're going to a private home, and bring a small gift. If you're invited out to a night on the town, be appropriately grateful, for your host is probably planning to spend a lot of money.

The Filipinos' style of entertaining is to invite you to a private home, where you and a gaggle of your host's friends will enjoy a lavish meal.

CHAPTER TWENTY-FOUR

A Communist Country

By the looks of it, in some ways, China is similar to the U.S. People get up, they go to work, and they live their lives just like we do. But, if you talk to the people there, and I mean genuinely, they will paint you a totally different picture.

If you read about Chinese history, you can follow how Communism came into existence there. The problem is not really that China is a Communist country. In my opinion, I would say that it is in the inequality of the Communist party. Most people that I got a chance to talk to about it told me that it was the blatant unfairness that pissed them off the most. The Chinese government has been known to take people's land away from them and then build them an apartment building in return. Many of these local farmers have no idea how to even operate a building, as they have no formal education.

It's hard to truly explain the culture in China, but for me it was like being in the movie "1984," but a little more relaxed. Communism came to power in 1949 under the power of Mao after the fall of Qing Dynasty. Communism began as a movement that paved the way for the liberation of the proletariat. Proletariat is a class of society that lives entirely from the sale of its labor and does not draw profit from any kind of capital.

After decades of civil war and invasion by Japan, the Communists under Mao prevailed. The opposition Nationalists fell and barely managed to retreat offshore to Taiwan. Over the years, China has continued to stay true to being a socialist state because it still regulates lending, especially to private companies, which often find it difficult to obtain credit or a loan for their ventures.

To this day, there are still protests that happen all over China. Protests are popular in China, but usually are short-lived because of the fear the people have from their government. The most famous protest in China happened in Beijing in June 1989. The Tiananmen Square protests of 1989, also known as the June Fourth Incident in Chinese, were student-led popular demonstrations that received broad support and exposed deep splits within China's political leadership. The protests called for government accountability, freedom of the press, freedom of speech, and the restoration of workers' control over industry. At the height of the protests, about a million people assembled in the Square.

On June 3rd and 4th, the military initiated martial law and attacked the protestors with assault rifles and tanks, inflicting thousands of casualties on unarmed civilians who were trying to block the military's advance on Tiananmen Square. Officially, the Chinese government condemned the protests as a riot and has prohibited all forms of discussion or remembrance of the events within China. A friend I met in Korea was actually detained in China because he was taking too many pictures in Tiananmen Square and had a postcard stating, "I will remember."

Internationally, the Chinese government was widely condemned for the use of force against the protestors. Most people still know very little, if anything, about the incident. In China today, children are taught the truth by their parents, and many sleeping dogs lie, waiting for the right reason to speak out.

At our local hangout, my friends and I would often end up talking to Chinese businessmen who would divulge their true feelings about the Chinese government and talk about the problems within their society. The weird part about it is that although they can be thrown in prison for speaking out, they still choose to in certain settings. I know in the U.S., people often can be found talking about politics, but we do have freedom of speech. In my impression of a lot of the Chinese people I encountered, I would say there is a strong underground liberal party.

If you ever visit China, I would suggest trying to keep quiet, and do not engage in these conversations until you know your surroundings. If you'll only be there a short time, you probably won't get a chance to have these sorts of discussions. But there are several thousand undercover police throughout the country. You never know who is listening.

Shanghai Tourism

Shanghai is a bustling mega-city with lots of history and great architecture. Just like Seoul, it lights up like a Christmas tree at night, but its skyline is by far much better to look at. There are hundreds of skyscrapers, and they all are different in size, shape and color. If you're looking for something to do, Shanghai is definitely the place to be. As an international city full of businessmen, tourists, and ESL teachers alike, there's something for everyone. While in Shanghai, I made it a point to make sure to see everything I could. I wasn't going to make the same mistake I made in Korea, and below are some of my favorites.

Shanghai literally means "the City by the Sea." It is located in central-eastern China, near the East China Sea, and has two different sections. The first section is Pudong, and Lujiazui is the part of Pudong located just after crossing The Bund and over the Huangpu River. This is the new section of Shanghai where most of the new skyscrapers are being built. There are many high-end restaurants here with beautiful views of the city skyline. Lujiazui is one of the four economic districts in Pudong. Be sure to check out the Oriental Pearl Tower, Jin

Mao Building, and Bank of China Tower. Definitely go to the Shanghai World Financial Center for a great night out and an amazing view of the city, or take a cruise on Huangpu River. It is only about four hundred meters wide and nine meters deep, but it holds about one-third of the China's total international trade. It supplies water to the thirteen million people in the metropolis and is also important for navigation, fishery, tourism and receiving wastewater. I don't suggest jumping in, as the water is extremely dirty.

The other section is Puxi, and it is located to the west of the Huangpu River. If you go to visit Shanghai, most of the historical and scenic places are in Puxi. There are many great places to visit in Puxi. One of the best places to check out is an area called The Bund. It stretches along the waterfront and is one of the most noted architectural symbols of Shanghai. It was first used when a British company opened an office there in 1846. It is now surrounded by about fifty various buildings of different architectural styles. This is also where you can catch the best view of Shanghai's skyline.

Another great place to visit is People's Square, which is located in the center of Shanghai. You'll most certainly end up here if you visit Shanghai, as it is the central subway station. People's Square is surrounded by the municipal government office buildings, the Shanghai Museum, Shanghai Exhibition Hall, and the Grand Theatre. There is also a huge park area with a smart musical fountain encircled by buildings on all sides that make up a beautiful view.

Perhaps my most favorite place is Shanghai was Yu Yuan Garden. The first reason I liked it so much was because it was a lot like my favorite street in Korea. The other reason was because of its famous gardens. It really is spectacular. Yuyuan is the most famous garden in Shanghai. It is located in the heart of Shanghai's Old City and is one of the few existent old tourist places in Shanghai. Directly next to it is a great number of small streets and lanes where vendors sell their products to the tourists and local people. "Yuyuan" literally means "peace and health" in Chinese, and the garden is nothing short of that. If you are looking for a peaceful journey followed up by a little shopping, Yu Yuan is the perfect place.

When it comes to going out on the town, you should definitely check out several places. Probably the most popular is The French Concession. In 1849, the French colonial officials created a district only for French people, and it became the city's best and most affluent residential area. The place was ruled by the French for nearly one hundred years until August 1943. The other is Xintiandi, and both places have several streets packed with bars, restaurants, clubs, stores, and street vendors. Xintiandi is similar to Lao Kwai Fong in Hong Kong. The French Concession is less condensed. There are many modern and new buildings around this old area, and it's a nice blend of the past and the present. You can find old traditional restaurants and new age bistros alike. Whatever fits your fancy, you can find here.

Shanghai's Nanjing Road is a walking street that is always packed with people watchers and is regarded as the first commercial road in Shanghai. It is the most bustling and prosperous street in Shanghai and now has turned into the number one site for shopping in the city. Nanjing Road extends from The Bund to Jing An Temple, and there are many modern shopping malls, specialty stores, theaters, and international hotels on both sides of the street.

I'm sure there are several other places that I didn't include, but you can easily check out several tourist sites. One thing I should mention to you is that China does have somewhat of a dark history that it tries to hide. There are places that only someone can tell you about, or how to get to. If something bad has happened there, you probably won't find it mentioned in a book or on a map. There were a few that I was told about, but I never got the chance to go to.

CHAPTER TWENTY-SIX

Beijing and the Great Wall of China

Looking West towards Mongolia, high on the peeks of the mountain tops.

On the top of my list before ever going to Asia was to visit and climb the Great Wall of China. It is one of the Seven Wonders of the World, and it seemed so intriguing to me, being the son of a general contractor. How could something so big be built over such a time period?

The Great Wall of China is a series of fortifications made mostly of stone, brick, and wood. It stretches from Shanhaiguan in the east to Lop Lake in the west, along an arc that roughly defines the southern edge of Inner Mongolia. It was generally built along an east-to-west line across the historical northern borders of China in part to protect the Chinese Empire. Several walls were being built as early as the 7th century BC. These later joined together and made bigger, stronger, and unified walls that are now collectively referred to as the Great Wall. The Great Wall has had many purposes that include but are not limited to border controls, trading, and control of immigration and emigration. The wall has been modified many times with defensive characteristics like watch towers, troop barracks, garrison stations, and signaling capabilities through the means of smoke or fire. It is also serves as a transportation corridor.

After three years in Asia, I finally was able to make my dream of seeing the Great Wall a reality. I had a week vacation from EF English First in October, and my friend Czarina and I decided to once again take a five-day trip together and go to Beijing. It was an inexpensive trip. A couple hundred dollars, really, for a plane ticket to Beijing and for the hotel, and then just spending money. We had a pretty good idea about what we wanted to do and see, and, for the most part, just wanted to relax.

Upon arrival in Beijing, it took us about an hour to get to our five-star hotel. Having Czarina as a travel companion had its perks. She was always great at finding deals on things like a hotel to save us money. However, when we got to the hotel, the staff told us they had no room available, even though we paid in advance. The hotel was overbooked, and the staff had to scramble to find us a room. It took them about an hour to prepare, upgrade us, and let us actually settle in our room for the night. Along with the room upgrade, they gave us a complimentary fruit and truffle basket. We were still annoyed, but what could one really do at that point? We went to bed early that night and rested up before heading to the Great Wall of China the next day.

The next morning I awoke to sound of Czarina blow-drying her hair and getting ready for our journey. I'm always groggy in the morning, but I grabbed some coffee and got ready. Czarina and I had breakfast in the hotel and then took the subway to the most northern point of Beijing near the Great Wall. From there, we took a taxi and made our hour trek to get to our destination. Czarina and I were dying with anticipation. We both had wanted to see the Great Wall of China and had discussed going many times in the past.

The area of the Great Wall we went to is called "North Pass" of Juyongguan Pass, also known as the Badaling. This area is very popular for tourists and is filled with peddlers and little shops carrying T-shirts, blankets, posters, and trinkets of all sorts. Since Czarina and I were experienced travelers, we knew that everything would be cheaper when we were leaving. We had to leave the same way and decided to wait until after to buy our souvenirs. So we made our way through and up to the gondola to take our ride up the mountain. The view was quite spectacular, as you could see for miles in every direction. It was also fall, so the trees were changing colors, and it really was very beautiful. After reaching the top, I think Czarina and I were both a little shocked. It's pretty hard to really grasp the size and magnitude of something so big, but there it was: the Great Wall of China.

Czarina and I spent the day walking along the wall and taking far too many pictures. We both exhausted our memory cards and had to put in new ones. My camera died at the end of the day with no power. The Great Wall is breathtaking and truly does leave you speechless. At the start of our day, there were several people on the wall with us, but as the day grew older, there were less and less people. We were able to take lots of unobstructed photos that we couldn't get earlier. We probably walked five miles in one direction that day and then five miles back, but it was well worth it. I to this very day look at my pictures of being there, and it still amazes me.

As the sun started to set that day, Czarina and I were just finishing our hike along the wall. We took the very last gondola ride down the mountain and then bartered with the little store owners to give us anything at a quarter of the price. I bought a T-shirt and a tapestry. Czarina bought a few other things. What would have cost us 1000 Yuan only cost us 200 Yuan. That is the difference of $150 to $30 USD. At the bottom of the mountain, we grabbed some sandwiches at Subway and called our taxi driver from before who was really cool and had a daughter who was studying English. He had her arrange it so he could pick us up and bring us back to our hotel as well. It worked out awesome, as we were really tired from a long day of hiking and climbing.

After making it back to the hotel, the two of us wanted nothing more than to lie down on our beds and rest up. Czarina had been saying all day that her back had been bothering her and that she wanted a massage. She called one and decided it was too expensive, but then after going to the hot tub saw a sign for another and decided to try that one. Maybe Czarina didn't quite understand what was about to happen, and neither did

I at first, but when in Asia, sometimes what you order is not what you get.

About an hour later as Czarina and I were watching a movie, there was a knock on the door. I was in my boxers and a T-shirt and went to answer the door. There before me was a Chinese girl wearing a bustier, the shortest mini-skirt I've ever seen, and fishnets. She was looking pretty hot, and I was totally shocked. I then knew what had happened, but I played it off and told Czarina her therapist was here to give her a massage. Many massage parlors in China are a disguise for brothels. For the next hour, I sat and watched in awe as this hot little Chinese girl massaged my friend. I'm also pretty sure she was trying to be erotic about it. She truly was bursting out everywhere, and it was impossible for me not to watch. I joked with Czarina after the hour was over, telling her what had just happened. Czarina just laughed, and said, "Really? She was pretty good!" The girl even asked me afterwards if I wanted a private massage. I knew what that meant and politely declined. Prostitution is prevalent in China, and especially in big cities. You have to be careful what you order.

For the next two days, Czarina and I traveled around the city. I continued to throw out one-liners about the hooker, and we continued to laugh about it. We went to all the places we could that were recommended by friends and by the travel books, but we ended up being disappointed. Beijing in my opinion is not a pretty city, nothing like Shanghai and its beautiful skyline. Beijing is basically a city of gray concrete. There is no skyline or unique architecture that I was able to see. There are a few notable places in the city to go see like The Forbidden City and Tiananmen Square, but that's really it. We went to both of these places, and I wasn't really impressed. I had seen far better temples and historic places in other cities and countries I had visited. The Forbidden City, although extremely big, was very poorly kept and maintained. It was also, along with Tiananmen Square, very busy and crowded with lots of people pushing and shoving to move. Due to the lack of places to check out in the city, we ended up just walking around most of the time and searching for things to do.

We went window shopping on our last day and looked through the markets for any cool trinkets we could find. There wasn't very much out there. Mostly what we found were cheap knock-offs that you could get just about anywhere in China. We ended up going to the Beijing Zoo, which was pretty good, even though under construction. Then, we called it a day early, returned to the hotel, and just relaxed by the pool and hot tub. It was great considering we had had a long couple of days. The next day we checked out and left Beijing in a plane back to Shanghai. It was a great trip, but only worth it once.

Conquests, KFC Anna, and the Taxi Cab Confessional

I couldn't write this book without telling you everything that went on while I was in Asia, so I have to share with you some of those crazy sexual escapades that happened over my four years abroad. I wouldn't say I'm the kind of person who goes on a conquest for ladies, but there were definitely a few women I had my eyes on over the years. Most of them never came into fruition, but that's how it was meant to be, I guess.

I had two serious girlfriends in Korea, but in between dating those two girls, I did have some fun going out with the boys. I had a few different circles of friends that I went out with. My main group of friends consisted of Bob, Josh, Brahm, Jiyeon, David, Rusty, Lynn, and multiple other people I knew through Toastmasters. Another group I hung out with was my friends Czarina, Jason, Sam, Thunder, Gaelan, a guy from Scotland named Thomas, and a smattering of others. In my first group of friends, we usually stuck to Hyehwa. It's where most of us lived, so it was easy, and we loved the fusion bar Comfort Zone due to being regulars and getting the occasional free drink or shot. Not to mention that we had crushes on most of the wait staff that worked there. In my second group, we tended to travel out more to the three major hotspots in Seoul. If you ever go to Seoul, South Korea, make sure you check out Itaewan, Gangnam, and Hongdae. These three places are where all the great clubs are, and it's not just one street. There are several blocks all together with four-story buildings with a club, bar, or restaurant on each floor.

Some of the funny things that we did in either group were to have theme nights when we all wore a wig, hat, or mustache. We also had nights when we had to use a certain line when talking to a girl. I remember one night in particular when we had to find a girl drinking a beer and say in either Korean or English, "Well, that's very unladylike of you!" I think everyone got slapped that night. There were many nights like that, some better than others, but we always had fun, and that was the point. In my first year, I still had hair and my friends used to always give me shit about it, saying I should just shave it all off. So one night when we were all wearing wigs, Czarina and I went back to Jason's house to polish off a couple bottles of good wine. Jason said, "Just let me shave it off!", and I said, "Sure, when you dress up in a clown costume." Jason laughed and walked away, while Czarina and I kept talking. Guess who just happened to have a clown costume in his closet? I haven't had hair since!

On Halloween one year I dressed up as David Bowie and had this crazy wig on. It seemed like every Korean girl had to try on my wig. One lady in particular that night made it a point to stay with the wig, if you catch my drift.

The two craziest and most unusual things that happened to me in Korea were KFC Anna and my taxi cab confessional. One day while doing some shopping in Sungshin, I stopped to get some food at KFC. I had been in Korea long enough to know how to order food, but the stupid adjushi behind the counter would not let me order. I tried ordering so many times that a line began to form. A Korean girl behind me started yelling at the adjushi and basically told him to stop being an asshole and give me my food. This was Anna, and I thanked her for helping me out. Later after finishing my meal, I walked up to her and gave her my business card. I thanked her and said, "Let me know if I can ever return the favor." Two days later around ten o'clock, I was out with my friends after a Toastmasters meeting for what we called second round. My phone rang, and there was Anna. She asked me to get together, and I had her meet me in Hyehwa. We went for a drink, and within about half an hour, she was all over me.

For about a month, we carried on with a sort of casual friend-with-fringe benefits relationship, but from day one, she seemed to not be dealing with a full deck. Each time we got together, it got weirder and weirder. There were times she would be waiting for me unannounced at 3 a.m. in front of my apartment. She would talk to me earlier, ask me what I was doing, and then just show up—sometimes sober, and other times barely able to stand. Even though she was cute in her own right, she really was crazy. One time when she was drunk, she took out two tables in a restaurant my friends and I were at, after just walking through the door. In the end, she was texting me every half-hour and calling me every twenty minutes. I had to change my number it was so bad.

My taxi cab confessional was how I met one of my best friends to this day. It is unfortunate my friend and I met this way, but that's the craziness of Korea. I had met Brendan and his girlfriend Christine about four months prior at a dinner party I was invited to by Josh. Christine and I hit it off because we both spoke French, but it was mostly just us joking around. I never saw her again until that summer when we were all out at the Comfort Zone. Christine just happened to be there and was looking fabulous. We got to talking and were having a good time when she whispered in my ear that she wanted me more than anything at that particular moment. I knew she had a boyfriend, so I said, "What happened to Brendan?" She told me they broke up and that he went back to Canada. I put on my sympathy face for a few minutes and then we of course went right back to deciding whose place we were going to go to. I asked my friends Bob and Josh about her, though, before continuing into anything, and they told me that as far as they knew she was single. I thought I was free and clear, but I would soon find out I was wrong.

Christine was a Kyopo, or Korean American to you. She was half American and Half Korean, born in America. She was also a little crazy, but not in a mental sense, more in a bedroom sense. There are some nights that will always have some sort of a stain on my brain. The one that I will always remember is when the two of us went to Hongdae for one of her friend's birthdays. We were both very drunk and at 3 a.m. were trying to get a taxi back to my apartment. We finally got one, and on the way back, Christine couldn't keep her hands off me. About five minutes into the ride, she got on top of me and we started going at it. The taxi driver actually turned his rearview mirror just so he could watch. When we got back to my apartment, we got out, and the taxi driver gave me a high five. Laughing, I paid him, and Christine and I walked up to my place.

It was a couple of days later that Josh and Bob approached me and told me that after talking to Brendan, they found out that he and Christine had never broken up.

I'm not the type of guy to go after someone else's girl, especially when he's friends with everyone I know. He was practically a part of my circle even though I wasn't friends with him. I immediately went and talked to Christine and broke everything off. When Brendan returned to Korea and I got the chance to see him, I pulled him aside and apologized. I explained everything to him, and all he said was, "Thank you. Maybe we can actually be friends."

Brendan and Christine obviously didn't stay together. Due to Toastmasters, and the fact that Brendan and I were friends with the same great group of people, we quickly became friends. There were a couple of times that Brendan and I were out together, and we saw Christine. Each time she turned and ran away, and Brendan and I laughed it off.

I'm not sure that I would have been so cool about it all, but that's the type of character Brendan has. It's also why I value his friendship so much. There are not many people in the world that can really see through all the bullshit and forgive people for their faults. He taught me a valuable lesson, I guess, and we're still good friends to this day.

Fighting for the Truth

On November 29, 2011, I had several different plans. The main plan was to attend my friend and co-worker Khanh's birthday party in Jing-an. I had to meet my friend Czarina at a bar called Windows Two in Jing An at 6 p.m. to give her a phone charger that she left in my apartment. After arriving at Windows Two, I bumped into a couple of friends and stayed for about an hour talking with them and catching up. I had one drink and then left to walk to my friend's birthday party at approximately 7 p.m.

Upon arriving at the party, I saw all my friends and co-workers. I ate some food and had a couple beers while socializing with everyone. Around 10 p.m. my friend Jonathan arrived and we continued to talk and socialize with the other guests until we left at 11 p.m. to go to I Club in Fuxing Park. We had been to I Club several times before due to being friends with the entertainment manager Yoyo, and he always took good care of us while we were there. This included copious amounts of alcohol and girls to keep us company. I had to work the next morning so I couldn't drink too much of the green tea and alcohol mixture that we always received.

My memory to this point in the evening is very clear. While in I Club, we were dancing, drinking, and having a good time. There was even one point at which I slipped in the club while dancing thanks to some guy bumping into me, but Jonathan helped me up. I was OK and just needed to catch my breath, but I decided to call it a night and said goodbye to Jonathan and left I Club at approximately 1 a.m. I remember getting my jacket, putting in my headphones, and leaving the club to retrieve a taxi to go home. I never made it out of the park. Unbeknownst to me, there were three Chinese men waiting for me around the corner.

As I was walking to get a taxi, listening to music on my headphones, I was struck very hard in the back of the head with something. Whether it was a fist, bottle, or rock, I'm not sure, but it was enough that I fell to the ground. It took a few seconds to sink in, but I was being attacked by a group of Chinese men. They were of average build. One was bigger than the other two. One was wearing white sneakers and an orange T-shirt. The others were wearing darker colors and black shoes. These three men were kicking me repeatedly while I was on the ground for about a minute or two. It was the longest two minutes of my life. You see things like this on TV, but you never expect them to happen to you. This was the real thing, and they were doing damage. After a couple of minutes, another man yelled, and the three attackers took off running. They did not rob me, if that was their intent. Maybe it was a hate crime, but I'll never truly know. The man came over and proceeded to help me up and asked me if I was OK. I can't remember more than that, or even my surroundings. I was truly out of it and in shock. I only remember him asking me if I was OK and where I lived. I remember getting into a taxi and going home.

The next morning, I woke up at approximately 8:30 a.m. I was in excruciating pain and couldn't move. It was the scariest feeling I've ever experienced. I truly thought I was having my last moments on this earth. It took me about 30 minutes to force myself to move and get my cell phone on my bureau across from my bed. I had to fall off my bed and crawl, all the while in excruciating pain. I then called my senior teacher, Samuel Evans, and then one of my bosses, Yihuai Cai. Neither of them answered their phone due to being in training, so I immediately called my friend Angel Chan and told her it was an emergency and I needed her to pick me up and take me to a hospital. She came to my apartment and rushed me to the nearest hospital, where I was admitted by the emergency room.

After a CT scan, X-rays, and an ultrasound, the doctors discovered that my spleen was ruptured, perforated, and bleeding badly. My appendix and gallbladder were crushed and needed to be removed. My liver was bruised and bleeding, and I had several bruised and cracked ribs. The doctors scheduled emergency surgery, but had to wait for blood to be flown in from Hong Kong because I had a rare blood type for China.

I was operated on later that evening, but before my surgery, my school director, Kenny Ye, along with the doctors, called the police and reported the incident. The police came to the hospital and, although they were actual officers in uniform, they were not from the right office and only asked some basic questions. The questions they asked that I can remember were "Where were you?" and "What happened?" I don't remember much of my response due to being heavily medicated at the time and I was just about to go into surgery. They also asked my friend Angel and my two bosses, Yihuai Cai and Kenny Ye, several questions.

The surgeons were able to save my spleen, but had to remove my appendix and gallbladder and also repair my liver. I would have to spend four weeks in the hospital and would need a minimum of another whole month to fully recover from the surgery, plus another four months after that to be back to normal.

What was about to transpire over the next several days—and still to this day—baffles me, but the police refused to allow me to make a true and accurate statement. They also continued to interrogate me while I was under the influence of extremely strong painkillers, including a morphine drip and Demerol. From Thursday to Saturday, the police or liaison officers came and questioned me several times. They were never in uniform, never identified themselves, and were very sneaky and cryptic every time they came. The police officers did have to sign in at the hospital desk, but you couldn't read their signatures. They tried to hide behind curtains and doorways, taped everything I said regardless of whether I was talking to them or not, and continually tried to change my story. It was so difficult to understand them because they kept talking in Chinese, and then asking me questions in broken English. The following is a day-by-day account of what the officers said and did.

THURSDAY, DECEMBER 1, 2011

Thursday was the first day of recovery for me after surgery. I was in and out of consciousness and recall only bits and pieces of the day. I do remember that the police came twice on Thursday. The first time, they came with my boss Kenny, who explained that they would ask me some question so they could investigate. There were two officers, a male and a female, and the male rarely spoke in English. They spoke with me about an hour, and my doctor asked them to leave, explaining I needed my rest. They came back several hours later, though, and continued to ask me several questions about the incident and were again asked to leave so that I could rest. I tried to refuse to answer their questions, but they were very persistent. I again want to make note of the fact that I was under the influence of narcotics painkillers at the time they were questioning me, and anything I said could be misconstrued due to the fact that I was at that time very intoxicated on pain medication.

On Friday, the police returned in the afternoon with my two bosses. There were three officers and the conversation started with my boss, Kenny, speaking me to cooperate with the police and tell them what they wanted to hear. Also of note, before the police came I was talking to my brother on Skype, and due to being incoherent, I forgot to end the call with him. He heard the entire interrogation, which lasted about an hour. It was on Friday that the police began to change their tune. They began asking me questions and changing the information. They did this by saying things like, "So two people attacked you outside of a McDonald's." They continued questioning me in a fast-paced manner with all three officers asking me questions at the same time. They were deliberate in nature and kept trying to get me to change my story. Even under the influence of strong medication, I did not change my story. The police kept saying over and over again, "We're trying to help you. Tell us the truth." I refused to change my story, got angry with them, and asked Kenny how I could let them question me like this. My direct supervisor, Yihuai, started crying and left the room. I did not see her again until over a week later after being discharged.

It got to the point where I was yelling at the police to leave my room because they kept trying to tell me that no one attacked me. The hospital staff, along with my surgeon, came and told them to leave. My surgeon instructed the hospital staff to not allow the police to talk to me anymore. Kenny, however, came into my room and tried to convince me to tell the police what happened. What he was really saying was things like, "Listen carefully to what the police tell you," "They are trying to help you so you don't go to jail," and, "Tell them you fell in the club and injured yourself." It was all very confusing for me, especially being under so much medication. I really didn't understand what was going on and why my boss was helping the police get me to change my story and say that nothing happened. He didn't speak English well enough for me to ask him.

The police returned again later that night after Kenny left and the hospital had its shift change. It was late, and the police woke me from sleeping. They continued with the same line of questioning, and I again asked them to leave. I told the police that I wasn't changing my story. I told them that I was attacked and that there was no way that I would change my story. The truth of the matter was they wanted me to lie to them and tell them nothing happened.

The next day, Saturday, I started receiving phone calls all day from one of the officers. The phone number is 1-381-791-5595. He must have called 20 times and sent me several text messages asking me to let him talk to me and saying he only wanted to help me. In the early afternoon, he, along with his translator, came into my hospital room and began with the same line of questioning. I continued to not change my story, and they got very angry with me. It was at this point that the male officer, who rarely spoke English during the questioning process, said to me, "Do you want to go to jail? You need to tell us the truth." I told them that I was telling the truth. They said that I wasn't listening and that they were trying to help me.

The male officer took out handcuffs and said, "Either you tell us what we want to hear, or you're going to go to jail."

I was very scared at this point. I still didn't really know what was going on. I asked them to leave again, and they did, but only after repeating several times that they were trying to help me.

After they left, my boss Kenny, came into the hospital room, sat next to my bed, and said, "Tim. You need to tell them that you injured yourself. Tell them that no one attacked you. If you tell them this, they will leave you alone and go away." I told him that I wasn't lying and that the whole situation was bullshit.

Thanks to my friends, I had not only contacted and spoke to attorneys at this point but also spoken with Paul, from the American consulate who had also visited me that Saturday in between when the police came. The second time the police came, I was talking with Paul and they ordered him to leave the room. After he left, they again continued to question me and tried to get me to change my story. I continued to refuse, but they continued to pressure me. They told me they wanted me to write down that I was not attacked and that I fell down and injured myself. They also told me that if I did not do this, they would return when I was stable and arrest me. They left and told me to seriously think about it.

I called my attorney and spoke to him about what was said. I was told that none of what I said during the questioning or anything I wrote would be legal because I was on medication and that I needed to be sober and completely coherent when making any testimony. This is also true in the U.S.: however, he did tell me that the police could throw me in jail if they felt I was a threat.

I decided that for my health and because I was in a Communist country, and they could put me in jail, I should just comply with their demands. I therefore wrote a brief statement stating that I was not attacked and that I injured myself falling down.

Later, two of my friends, Joshua Davies, an American with whom I was friends with in Korea, and another friend, Natalie, were visiting me. While they were there the male police officer called and asked me if I would write the statement. I told them yes and he came back to the hospital with the female translator. I gave them the written statement, but they didn't like it and wanted me to rewrite it. I did so and the conversation was all recorded on my iPhone. The police did not know that they were being recorded telling me what they wanted me to write. You can hear them halfway through in the background telling me what to do. My friends couldn't even believe what transpired in front of them and told me I should hire an attorney to sue them for the injustice they were doing. Unfortunately, after talking with several attorneys, I was told that trying to prosecute a police officer was next to impossible and very expensive.

Paul returned later that evening, and we discussed what happened. I told him that I was completely disgusted with the police, my boss, the incident, and everything that happened.

It was at this time that I decided to not keep quiet, to make sure the truth was told, and to make sure that everyone knew what really happened to me. I also wanted justice for what happened to me. Knowing that I was leaving the country and going home, I had decided to have the American consulate investigate the matter. It was for that reason that I wrote everything down and sent it to the every newspaper I could find an email for. Unfortunately, it was never published due to the fear of an international incident. Every newspaper in China and the U.S. that responded told me that they couldn't publish the story. I also later found out, after being released from the hospital, that the American consulate office has absolutely no power to investigate anything. It only has the power to say it wants a matter investigated.

After all that I had been though, I was in total disgust over the entire situation. It still pisses me off to this day when I think about it, or when I look in the mirror and see my scar. I almost died after being attacked by three Chinese men. No one, in any country, should have to endure what I went through, but I lived to tell about it, and that's what matters.

CHAPTER TWENTY-NINE

A Curtain Call:
Leaving Asia and Steps for the Future

One of my favorite trips to the Islands in Korea with Sinchon Toastmasters

On December 24, 2011, I left Asia for the final time. I was released from the hospital a few days earlier, but was told to be on bed rest for the next thirty to forty-five days. Needless to say, I was still in recovery at the time, and thankfully a few of my friends helped me pack all my things and mail boxes home. If you were to have seen me, I pretty much looked like an emaciated walking zombie, high on Oxycontin, and clueless as to my own reality. On my last night in Shanghai, I got together with the few friends I had made there and said my goodbyes. In some ways, I was sad to leave, but in most regards, I was happy to leave the Communist Red China.

Due to the circumstances of my injuries, the aftermath with my boss, and the police, I was asked to leave China quietly by not only my family, who wanted me home safe, but also my friends and also a representative from the Chinese police. I negotiated and was given a settlement to keep my mouth shut. I can't discuss the exact amounts or details of it, but I can say it was enough for me to leave and be OK with it. I had them by the balls, anyway. I had my boss and the police on tape telling me to change my story and lie about what happened to me. Everything was recorded, including their threats to throw me in jail if I didn't comply. I honestly just wanted to get the hell out. Who wants to stay in a country that is unsafe and where it's OK to attack people because of the color of their skin? When I think about it, I know it could have happened anywhere, but at least it would be investigated in the U.S.A.

Flying out of Shanghai was probably the worst flight of my life. When my flight was bought through Air Canada, it was arranged for me to have a wheelchair, help with my baggage, and special seating so I could be comfortable. My mother set it up long before I even was released from the hospital. Somehow all of this got terribly messed up. No one helped me with my luggage, except the taxi driver that was arranged by my friend Angel. That only got me inside the airport, though. When I tried to check in, the airline staff told me I had to pay extra money for my baggage. I told them that I had pre-paid for extra baggage and that my whole itinerary and medical status had been pre-established. They said that no information was in the system, that I had to pay for extra baggage and carry it myself, and that my seat had been moved. I not only was off my rocker at this point in time, but I also pretty much threw a fit in the middle of the airport terminal demanding that they fix my status back to what it was. They, of course, called airport security and I had to explain the situation. Eventually, they called Air Canada and I was put back on special status, but I still had to pay for my extra baggage, and I lost my special seating and was moved next to some orca-fat guy in the back of the plane that smelled like he rolled himself in pig shit before getting onboard. I proceeded to take several of my prescribed pills and pass out. Luckily, I did sleep most of the way, but it was a long fourteen hours to Toronto, and when I did need to get out of my seat, climbing over the orca-fat pig shit guy proved to be quite difficult.

True to fashion, when I arrived in Toronto, there was no wheelchair waiting for me, and I had 20 minutes to catch my plane to Boston. I wasn't going to get stuck in Toronto for five days, so I did everything I could, including paying people to help me with my baggage. I was able to get my bags onto a baggage cart, but a few minutes later was told that I had to carry my bags because the baggage carts weren't allowed through customs. I was so pissed off at this point that I lifted my shirt and gave the guy the finger. I then waited in line for about 30 minutes to go through customs and get on the plane. Air Canada did one thing right after screwing everything else up, because it held the plane for me and eight other passengers.

Once I made it through customs, you'll never believe what happened. There was actually a flight attendant standing there with a wheelchair. The boarding gate was less than 100 feet away. The attendant demanded that I sit in the chair and wait for everyone else to get on the plane. I said no, but she said, "Sit or stay in Toronto for five days." I just shut up and did what she asked. When I got onto the plane, the same flight attendant asked me if there was going to be a problem and suggested I take another flight. I just completely ignored her and closed my eyes.

Three hours later, I arrived in Boston. When leaving the plane, I told the flight attendant to go fuck herself and that I hoped she choked on the piece of coal she got for Christmas. My parents were waiting for me at the terminal, and I was finally home. It was a long ordeal, but I made it home and I was safe.

Over the next several months, I continued with my recovery and started trying to rebuild my life in the U.S.A. It was a rude awakening to be home. Nothing seemed the same, and finding a job was tough. I thought it would be easier and that I'd find a marketing job somewhere near Boston. I eventually found my place, though, and invested in a driving school. I presently am a partner, program director, and certified driving instructor. It surely wasn't what I expected to be doing, but I love it. I guess teaching really is my calling.

EPILOGUE

It was my pleasure to write about my experiences while teaching and traveling through Asia. I hope you enjoyed looking through the hourglass at my crazy cultural experiences and misunderstandings. Even now, looking back on everything that happened, I wouldn't change a single moment of it. It might be better to say that I wish I could take back being attacked in China, but if I had to experience that so I could do everything else, I think I would do it all over again.

I think about my experiences abroad every day. It is quite often that I find myself laughing, remembering something that happened, or telling someone a story about one crazy night. I know I would love to go back to Asia, but not for the same reasons. I have so many friends all over the world now that I never had before, and several are still in Korea and China. I keep in touch with most people here and there, and we try to get together when possible. Even though I loved teaching ESL, I like having my own business in the U.S., and I missed my friends and family too much when I was gone. There truly is no place like home. I know that one day, however, I plan to retire someplace tropical like Thailand or Costa Rica.

The lifelong lessons I've learned have made me the person I am today, and I'm surely better for it. I truly needed to learn more about myself and the world around me. I always wanted to travel and see the world, and now that I have, I'm sure I'll be traveling again soon.

Thanks again for reading *ASIA: An Expat Adventure*. If you found this book helpful and would like to purchase additional copies, or you would like to contact the author, please visit http://www.expat-adventures.com.

NOTES

1. Min Byoung-chul, Ed.D., *Ugly Koreans, Ugly Americans: Cultural and Behavioral Differences Between Koreans and Americans.* BCM Media, Inc, 2005

2. Meier, Michael, MBA. *A Focused Pursuit In China: 14 Business Tips Before You Go.* Maximizer World Publishing, 2010.

3. http://en.wikipedia.org/wiki/Korea

4. http://en.wikipedia.org/wiki/Shanghai

5. http://en.wikipedia.org/wiki/China

6. http://en.wikipedia.org/wiki/Tokyo

7. www.culural-china.com

8. http://www.tour-beijing.com/shanghai_travel_guide/

9. http://en.wikipedia.org/wiki/Great_Wall_of_China

10. http://www.blackoutkorea.com

11. http://en.wikipedia.org/wiki/Tiananmen_Square_protests_of_1989

12. http://en.wikipedia.org/wiki/English_as_a_second_or_foreign_language

INDEX

ABOUT THE AUTHOR

Born and raised just outside of Boston in a small city, Timothy Marc Pelletier has achieved a level of success few would have expected: At the age of 12, Timothy's school psychologist told his parents he would never make it past the eighth grade. Taking this in stride, Timothy learned a valuable life lesson and became determined to never let anything get in his way. He has endured many struggles throughout his life, including being partially paralyzed in a car accident at the age of 18. At the age of 29, he gave up everything he owned in search of a new beginning in Seoul, South Korea. Now at age 34, he has become a leader amongst the community, and is currently the managing partner of his own company.

In his free time, Timothy enjoys traveling more than anything else. He has visited more than 30 countries learning about culture and people; speaks Mandarin Chinese, Korean, French, and English: and is always looking for his next adventure. With several years of business experience and international travel, Timothy is a trainer/speaker who offers a wealth of knowledge on how to overcome the obstacles in our everyday life.

You can contact Timothy at
http://www.expat-adventures.com
and follow him on Twitter @ ExpatAdventures